D0944679

# KING AND MESSIAH

# KING AND MESSIAH

AAGE BENTZEN

*Edited by*
G. W. ANDERSON

BASIL BLACKWELL OXFORD

First published by Zwingli Verlag, Zürich

First English edition 1955 by the Lutterworth Press, London
Second edition 1970

0 631 12850 6
Library of Congress Catalog Card No.: 78-122580

Printed in Great Britain for BASIL BLACKWELL & MOTT, LTD.
by COMPTON PRINTING LTD., London and Aylesbury
and bound at the KEMP HALL BINDERY

# FOREWORD

It is unnecessary to introduce Aage Bentzen to Old Testament scholars in any country. Apart from the fact that he published a long array of books and articles, not only in the Danish language, but also in English, German and French, the fact that he was elected the first President of the International Old Testament Organization, which was formed at Leiden in 1950 and held its first Congress at Copenhagen in 1953, indicates the sure place he had in the affection and esteem of his fellow scholars of all countries. Only a few weeks before the meeting of the Congress to which he had so looked forward and for which he had worked so hard he died an untimely death at the age of fifty-eight.

To me he was not only a fellow scholar, but an intimate friend, and it is a melancholy duty to write a Foreword to the book of one I loved so well. I met him first at the International Meeting of the Society for Old Testament Study held in Cardiff in 1946, though many letters had passed between us before that date. Both of his daughters have paid visits to my home, and I have more than once been the guest in his home. To many of the members of the Society for Old Testament Study he gave his friendship, and they share the warmth of my feelings on every remembrance of him. Only a few months before his death the Society elected him one of its Honorary Members.

Few men worked harder or wrote more than Bentzen. Many of his works are text-books produced in Danish for his own students. One of these, his *Introduction to the Old Testament*, has been translated into English and has already gone into a second edition. He was not primarily an original scholar. His mind was less creative than those of several of the other Scandinavian Old Testament scholars of the present time. On the other hand, he was never a mere mediator of the ideas of others. He brought his own contribution to what he received from others, and above all he brought a balanced judgment which kept him from going to any of the extremes of interpretation.

These qualities are well seen in the present work, which mediates to non-Scandinavian readers something of the ferment of ideas which has marked Scandinavian scholarship in recent years, and which at the same time offers its contribution to the inner-Scandinavian discussion of the issues. English readers will value it most because it makes available to them so much of the discussion which has taken place in the Scandinavian languages, and will give them some clear guidance through the streams of Scandinavian patternism as applied to the "messianic" ideas of the Old Testament.

H. H. ROWLEY

Manchester, 1954

## AUTHOR'S PREFACE

THIS book was first published in German by the Zwingli-Verlag in Zürich in the year 1948, as vol. 17 of the *Abhandlungen zur Theologie des Alten und Neuen Testaments*, edited by Eichrodt and Cullmann. In the Preface to this first edition I underlined its sketchy and fragmentary character, and I expressed my hope that it might serve as some sort of information on contemporary Scandinavian discussions and that my own statements might carry our work on the Old Testament forward, even if it were through its provocation of antagonistic criticism. When it is now translated into English, and—as I hope—also into the Czechoslovakian tongue, I can only hope that this will serve the same ends.

I have tried to bring it up to date by references to more recent literature, and some alterations have also been introduced into the argument. But essentially it is the same book as the German edition.

I thank the Reverend E. W. Heaton, M.A., Fellow of Gonville and Caius College, Cambridge, for his help in correcting the English translation so that readers will be able to get a clearer idea of my opinions.

AAGE BENTZEN

Hellerup, 1953

# FOREWORD TO SECOND EDITION

In the years immediately following the Second World War, "Sacral Kingship" was probably the most hotly debated subject in the entire field of Old Testament religion. The ramifications of the debate included the influence on Israel of ancient Near Eastern culture and religion, the interpretation of the Psalms, the development of the Messianic hope, the identity of the Suffering Servant of Yahweh, and the origin and nature of the concept of the Son of Man. When the present book first appeared in German (1948) and in a revised and enlarged form in English (1955), it provided a valuable guide to the Scandinavian contributions to the debate. Aage Bentzen was peculiarly well fitted to write such a book. As the late Professor Rowley pointed out in his foreword to the first English edition, his judgement was balanced and he was not an advocate of extreme views. Moreover, as the author of substantial commentaries on the Psalms (*Fortolkning til de gammeltestamentlige Salmer*, Köbenhavn, 1939) and Isaiah (*Jesaja, fortolket*, I–II, Köbenhavn, 1943–4) and of a shorter commentary on Daniel (*Handbuch zum Alten Testament*, I, 19, Tübingen, 1937, ²1952), he had already undertaken an independent examination of most of the Old Testament passages which are relevant to the debate.

Since 1955 the centre of interest in the study of Old Testament religion has to some extent shifted. But the King-Messiah and the Suffering Servant can never be far from the heart of any balanced presentation of the faith of Israel; and if the religious thought of the intertestamental period and of the Gospels is included in the perspective, then the Son of Man problem must also come under review. Bentzen's book retains its value, because it summarizes his own considered opinions on these themes.

No attempt has been made in this new edition to bring the documentation up to date. To have done so would have encumbered a relatively short book with a weight of bibliographical apparatus which is readily available elsewhere, e.g., in the volume *Myth, Ritual and Kingship*, ed. by S. H. Hooke (Oxford, 1958), in the second edition of Professor A. R. Johnson's *Sacral Kingship in Ancient Israel* (Cardiff, 1967), and in

the supplementary bibliography in the second edition of I.
Engnell's *Studies in Divine Kingship in the Ancient Near East*
(Oxford, 1967). Some slight modifications have, however, been
made in the notes. References to S. Mowinckel's *Han som
kommer* (Köbenhavn, 1951) have been replaced by those to the
English translation, *He That Cometh* (Oxford, 1956, ²1959); and
in the few places in the notes where Bentzen quoted this work
verbatim, giving his own English rendering of Mowinckel's
Norwegian text, the rendering of the English edition is now
printed. Similarly, references to F. F. Hvidberg's *Graad og
Latter i det Gamle Testamente: en Studie i kanaanaeisk-israelitisk
Religion* (Köbenhavn, 1938) are now replaced by those to the
English translation, *Weeping and Laughter in the Old Testament:
a Study of Israelite Religion* (Leiden and Köbenhavn, 1962). O.
Eissfeldt's *Einleitung in das Alte Testament unter Einschluss der
Apokryphen und Pseudepigraphen* (Tübingen, 1934, ²1956, ³1964),
which Bentzen referred to in its first edition, is now cited
according to the English translation, *The Old Testament: an
Introduction* (Oxford, 1966), abbreviated as *Introduction*. On the
other hand, references to the Swedish version of I. Engnell's
article on the Suffering Servant ("Till frågan om Ebed-Jahve-
sångerna", *S. E. Å.*, x, 1945, pp. 31–65) have been left unaltered.
The English version ("The 'Ebed Yahweh Songs and the
Suffering Messiah in 'Deutero-Isaiah' ", *B. J. R. L.*, 31, 1,
1948) contains a number of differences from the original. For
the most part Bentzen quoted from the English version; but his
references to the Swedish text were deliberately made because
of the differences just mentioned; and to alter them would
obscure the points which he wished to make.

The style of documentation adopted by Bentzen was not
entirely consistent; but since his references are sufficiently
clear, the minor inconsistencies have not been eliminated.

Aage Bentzen's memory is still cherished by those who were
privileged to know him as colleague and friend. The present
work is reissued in the hope that it will not only meet a demand
which has been expressed in many quarters, but also mediate
something of Bentzen's work to a new generation of students of
the Old Testament.

G. W. ANDERSON

Edinburgh, 1969

# CONTENTS

# 1

## INTRODUCTION

It will be generally known that the approach to the Psalms of the Old Testament has changed considerably during the first half of the twentieth century.[1] This change is especially obvious on the European continent.[2] The form-critical and religio-historical outlook, inaugurated by Hermann Gunkel and developed in a more simple and consistent manner by Mowinckel, is the scientific foundation of this new development. The Psalms now are regarded not only formally, but also materially, as part of the religious poetry of the Ancient Near East. The religio-historical interpretation of the Psalms as cultic poetry was deepened through the fertile ideas of Vilhelm Grönbech,[3] and these have influenced Mowinckel as well as other scholars—especially Danish ones. Mowinckel's interpretation of the so-called "Ascension-Psalms" (primarily Psalms 47, 93 and 95–100) is an adaptation of Grönbech's ideas.

The Festival of Yahweh's Ascension to his Throne on New Year's Day, which Mowinckel finds reflected in these and related psalms, is described on the lines of a "ritual drama" with the re-creation of the world as its central theme.[4] In the ritual drama of the New Year Festival at the time of the autumn equinox, Israel experienced a repetition of the events at the Creation of the world—God's fight against the powers of Chaos, the primeval ocean, Rahab, the Dragon and their attendant host of demons. This Divine fight ends in the defeat of the enemies of God and precedes the creation of the heavenly vault as the strong protection against the powers of Chaos, the "Sea" and the "Flood". The creation of the Heavens is God's decisive act of salvation and the proof of His power over all other gods. "All gods of the nations are mere idols, but the Eternal made the heavens".[5] In the festival, this act of salvation was re-experienced by the people, through the religious act of "remembrance", *anamnesis*.[6] "To remember" the saving facts of religion means to the Ancient World that these facts are tangibly experienced, that the members of the congregation, to use an expression from Kierkegaard, "become contemporary" with the fundamental act of salvation in the history of the world. The religious experience involved is best illustrated from the Roman Mass and the Lutheran interpretation of the Communion Service, as expressed in Grundtvig's version of the Latin hymn on the "sweet remembrance" of Jesus, which has nearly become a part of the Danish Communion ritual. When Christ is properly remembered, He is actually present as a living reality. The Creation of the Heavens, the Divine fact of Salvation, is phenomenologically and typologically[7] a parallel to the *"consummatum est"* of the New Testament. It is the Divine act through which the life of the people of God is assured.

This conviction is most impressively set forth in the sublime lines of the *Eighth Psalm*. The poet contemplates the Heavens as the bulwark created by the Lord against all his enemies. This work of Yahweh is greater than any other work of His, even greater than the First Man, who was created to be King of God's World. But this contemplation of the works of God is expressly the re-experience of the Salvation, in its ritual re-iteration. It fills the souls of the worshippers with the assurance that "God's in his Heaven—All's right with the world". The World stands again—firm over the threatening Flood. Chaos cannot hurt God's people. This assurance is found not only in Psalm 8 and (for example) in Psalm 93, but also in Psalm 29 and in the great hymn which Luther "christened" —Psalm 46.

The Ascension-and-New-Year Festival of Israel, which emerges from the Old Testament hymns, was related to similar celebrations all over the Ancient Near East.[8] Mowinckel in his *Psalmenstudien II* certainly compared the Israelite festival and its Babylonian counterpart; but he did not, as is often said, take his starting point in Babylon. He started in Israel, as good method demands.[9] Paul Volz had already trodden this path, but Mowinckel worked more consistently and, above all (thanks to Grönbech), he had a more lively understanding of the religious experience found in the festival. Mowinckel's description was then enriched through the great finds of the Ras Shamra "mythological" tablets. Flemming Hvidberg's investigations[10] of these texts have shown that the Divine Ascension Festival was found also in Canaan. We now perceive (as the British so-called "Myth and Ritual School"[11] has also maintained) that a "ritual pattern", in many variations, but with certain essential features, appears in various parts of the Ancient East and seems to be important for the understanding both of Old Testament ritual and ecclesiastical cult and dogma.

In this connection, the figure of the *divine* or *sacral king* has attracted special interest. Swedish scholars, as earlier the Danish Johs. Pedersen, have emphatically stressed the position of the king in the cult as the vicegerent of the god, as "son of the god", who fights the god's fight in the ritual drama of the creation festival. Like Ba'al, he suffers death and is raised from the underworld, and so secures salvation for the people which he embodies. In Canaan, the Death and Resurrection of the god are integral elements of the cultic drama. These ideas were accepted by Israel only in a severely modified form. The "dying god", as Johs. Pedersen, Hvidberg and Engnell unanimously assert, was incompatible with Israel's idea of God. Yahweh was eminently the "Living God", "the God of Life", the God "who does not die", as the original text of Habakkuk 1:12 runs according to rabbinical tradition. But this conviction did not prevent certain features from the ritual combat between God and the powers of Chaos, as we see it in poetical allusions in Job, the Prophets, above all in Deutero-Isaiah, from entering the world of Israelite thought.

The myth of the fight of the gods was, however, fundamentally reinterpreted in Israel. Above all, it was "historified" and, in the Passover ritual, turned into a myth of God's fight against the "nations". The Chaos, Rahab and Tiamat were identified with Egypt and Pharaoh, and the legend of the Exodus was embellished by features drawn from the Creation epic.[12] This has been especially emphasized by Johs. Pedersen. Features from these mythical complexes are present in great numbers in the Psalms, especially in those we call the "Royal Psalms". These "Royal Psalms" are now generally treated, not as political and historical documents, but as cultic ritual poems. Even when elements from the mythical combat are found in poems which are perhaps better understood politically and historically, they are, nevertheless, to be recognized as survivals from the earlier "pattern". Political enemies and the military defeats of the king are described and painted in colours taken from the divine ritual combat. The political enemies are identified with the powers of Chaos; the powers of Chaos are actualized in political enemies.

There are psalms other than those which are expressly labelled "Royal Psalms" because they mention the king, the Anointed of the Lord, etc., which belong to this material. In agreement with an idea which is common among historians of religion, recent scholars (especially in Sweden) have emphasized that the Psalms in general, in Israel as among other peoples, originally belonged to a royal ritual. Later, it is said, they were "democratized", that is, the rituals were made accessible to the general public, the "commoners". In Israel, this is especially the case with the poems which have as their subject the innocent suffering of the servant of God (Psalms 22, 69, etc.). It is clear that the problem of the "enemies" in the Psalms must be re-studied in the light of this new approach. In many cases, we shall probably have to conclude that the "enemies" in the Psalms (even in those where the king is not explicitly mentioned) are primarily the powers of Chaos, the primeval enemies of men and God, who are conquered by the sacral king. In some psalms, however, they have been actualized in the concrete enemies of the nation or of the single individual, whether they be demons, or men who have made a covenant with them, "sorcerers", or whatever else combats the plans of the saving God of the Creation Story.

Of course, we must never forget the strong influence on all such foreign ideas which was exercised by the Israelite conception of the "jealous God" of Moses. This is especially obvious in the sphere of Creation-ideology. What people meant, when they heard the words of Psalm 95: 5, it is not easy to say. The "Sea" to most of them would recall the evil power of *tᵉhôm*, the Flood, and similar malignant primeval monsters. When it is said that God "made" it, an idea quite different from that given by the ancient myths may have been conveyed. It seems that the "Sea" has been "depotentialized" through the Israelite belief that God has all powers in His hands. He "made" even the Chaos. Or did men distinguish, in a case like this, between the primeval monstrous "Sea" and the sea of the ordered universe after the third day of Creation? The parallelism of 95: 5 seems to favour this interpretation. But, at all events, the psalm is tending towards a comprehensive monism, with Yahweh as the sole agent in Creation and with all the powers subordinated to Him. This, however, does not exclude the significance of the "parallels" drawn from the other spheres of the Ancient Near East. Although they are reinterpreted when taken up into the Israelite cultural structure, it is of importance to know whence Israel got the material by means of which its culture was built up.

# 2

## THE MESSIAH IN THE PSALMS

*The Second Psalm*

ACCORDING to the conception outlined in the introductory
chapter, the Psalms—or at least many of them—should be
understood primarily as representing the fate of the sacral
king and the people whom he impersonates in the important
rites of the New Year Festival. Against this background, Psalm
2 is taken to describe the situation in which the king challenges
God's enemies, the Chaos and its demonic powers, and gives
his last warning before starting to fight them.

The usual interpretation of the psalm, however, suggests
that it is an oracle on the day of the king's ascension to his
throne. This interpretation should not be abandoned in favour
of the new idea, but rather developed more elaborately, in the
light of our new knowledge about the kings of the Ancient
East. The presupposition is that the Day of the Ascension to
the Throne is no common day of the year. The kings of Babylon
and Assyria do not ascend the throne *de jure*, until the New
Year's Day following the death of their predecessor; and in
Egypt the coronation of the king takes place in connection with
the *beginning* of the rule of the gods.[1] The Mesopotamian idea
of the *reš šarruti*, i.e. the period between the death of the old
king and the New Year Festival inaugurating the first year of
the new king's reign, was also known in Israel, at least about
600 B.C. (Jeremiah 26: 1; cf. 27: 1 and 28: 1).[1a]

In the New Year Festival, the repetition of Creation also
takes place, re-enacted in the cultic drama.[2] The enemies
mentioned in the psalm, the *gôyîm*, "the nations", "the kings
of the earth", etc., are "historifications" of the demonic
powers of Chaos from the myths of the fight of the gods or of
the fight between God and the nations. When the ritual was
enacted, men of course actualized it in relation to the enemies
of their own time. So far, then, it is true that this psalm reflects

as well the typical situation at the death of a king and the ascension of another. It is then that vassal and satellite states and subjugated nations plan to throw off the yoke of the tyrants and become independent. But this historical presentation should be interpreted as an actualization of a situation known at the time of the Creation, when the Chaos was conquered by the saving acts of God and his Anointed.

The enthronement of a king is always a repetition of a primeval act. It is a repetition of the enthronement of the first king in the days of the beginning, the primeval age. The first king is the patriarch of the Royal House, identical with the patriarch of mankind.[3] Hammurabi says in the introduction to his great collection of Babylonian Laws that he got his "name" from the great Creators Anu and Enlil, when they created the World; i.e. that *he was elected* king at the creation.[4] The same is said in Israel of the Messiah in Micah 5: 1, where his epiphany is compared with the sunrise (*môṣâ'ôtâw*, cf. Psalm 19: 7 and Luke 1: 78, *anatolé*).[4a] And so we get a significant and powerful pun between the two meanings of the word *mikkedem*: "His uprising is from the East", the latter word (*mikkedem*) being interpreted in its other sense through *mîmê 'ôlâm*, "from the Days of Old", the beginning of time.[5] The Messianic poem in Micah 5, like the parallels in Isaiah 9 and 11, is a typical Royal Psalm. This conception of the primeval election and birth of the king is also preserved in the ancient versions of Psalm 110: 3 (cf. LXX, Syr. and also Vulg.)[6] Probably this same idea is behind the name of the Messiah in Isaiah 9: 5, when he is called not only "God Almighty", but also *'abî-'ad*, "Father from Eternity", i.e. "primeval patriarch".

The king, then, is *Primeval Man*. The first man of Genesis 1: 26–28 is described as the first ruler of the world. In the first Creation Story, the "gospel" of the New Year, we hear the blessing spoken by God at the enthronement of the first Royal Couple of the world. Man is to "rule" over all living creatures. Man and Woman, like the Babylonian kings, are "images of God", i.e. the Royal Couple is Divine, as in the famous apostrophe to the king in the oracle for the Royal wedding (Psalm 45: 7). The same idea is developed in Psalm 8, in the description of the "Son of Man", who is "little lower than God",

B

"nearly a God". This "Son of Man", according to the evident dependence of the psalm on the ideas behind the first chapter of Genesis, is the First Man and the First King. Widengren has rightly pointed out[7] that the same ideas are found in the Creation story of Genesis 2: 4ff., where we are told that the First Man gave the animals their names and that none of them was his equal. (I note in passing that it is not *quite* relevant for Mowinckel to say that Primordial Man is not called "King" in late Jewish speculations on Adam.)[8] Of the other descriptions of First Man in the Old Testament (Ezekiel 28: 1–10, 11–19 and Job 15: 7f.), at least the first points to a king. Ezekiel here uses the mythical ideas in describing the Tyrian king, who dwells on "the seat of the gods", just as the Israelite prince in Psalm 110 is enthroned at the right hand of God, on Zion, his holy mountain (Psalm 2).[8a]

The enthronement of the king in Primeval Time is also described in the second psalm in the very much discussed particle '*âz* in v. 5.[9]

It has been debated whether this particle should be interpreted as retrospective or prospective. I think the first alternative is the right one, but it has a special nuance. The word is used in a pregnant sense, pointing here (as in many Old Testament passages) to some fundamental event, and with a sort of prophetic *chiaroscuro* veiling its deep meaning:[10] "Then —you know when . . . !" In the same manner, the particle points back to the election of the Davidic dynasty in Psalm 89: 20. In the Enthronement Psalms, it is used of the acts of salvation in the drama of Creation in Psalm 96: 12 and in Psalm 93: 2, where it is interpreted through the parallel *mê 'ôlâm*. In Exodus 9: 24, it is used of the primeval days of Egypt. In Deutero-Isaiah, whose style is so extraordinarily influenced by the Enthronement Psalms, we also meet the pregnant, allusive meaning of the word. In 44: 8, it points to the Call of Israel, which, of course, is an event from Primeval Days, because the salvation of the people at the Exodus from Egypt was identified with the Creation. In 45: 21, it is used in parallelism to *mikkedem*, again pointing to the connection with the Creation (cf. Micah 5: 2). This meaning is also most probable in 48: 5, 7, 8. The reference in Psalm 76: 8 must be regarded in the same light as 96: 12. Again, Proverbs 8: 22 quite distinctly speaks of the Creation. The entire verse (especially the expressions *kedem*, *mê 'ôlâm* and *mêrô'š*) is decisively in favour of this interpretation. Finally, the terminology of the Creation myth completely determines the situation of Psalm 124, where the word occurs several times in the form *'azaj*.[11]

From these indications, I think it is comparatively clear that *'âz* in Psalm 2 as well as in 89: 20 must be interpreted as pointing to the election of the Royal house at the time of the Creation.[12] "Then", in the primeval morning, when the devils of the Chaos came together in order to vanquish Yahweh and his Anointed (vv. 1–3), "*then*" the heavenly king of Israel hurled his mighty word of creation against them. This is repeated now. Yahweh treats them with laughter and scorn. He has taken measures to keep them down. He has enthroned his King in the Sanctuary of Jerusalem, which is also from the Days of Old (cf. e.g. Jeremiah 17: 12). This king and saviour, who (like all ancient kings) is also his prophet,[13] now pronounces the will of God, God's ultimatum to the rebels, and warns them to turn back before it is too late.

The king, as in Mesopotamia, is *Son of God*[14] by *adoption*.[15] Scholars generally agree that the king of Israel has been invested with the same divine qualities as elsewhere in the Ancient East. Although certain expressions, especially in vv. 4–7, remind us very much of the text II AB VIII, 42–52 from Ras Shamra, it is probable that the Psalm in Israelite use has not gone as far in identifying the Son of God with God as did the Canaanite ritual. Israel may well have stressed the idea of adoption; and, of course, we also have to reckon with many different shades of opinion in Israel. But we have no right at all to doubt that in principle the king of Israel was considered an *'elôhîm*.[16] We may add that in Israel there seems to have been a strong tendency to "Nestorianism"—if we may speak in ecclesiastical-dogmatic terms. But the king is thought of as the divine-human bearer of salvation, the guarantor of the victory of God. He is not so absolutely a god as in Egypt.

It is certainly significant, too, that in Psalm 2 the enemies are described as "terrestrial" ("kings of the earth", v. 2). These earthly beings are emphatically confronted with "Him that sits in the heavens" and we find the king on his side through the divine act of adoption. Through the ceremony of anointing, and through the enthronement mentioned in v. 6, he has been made "celestial". He is now, through God's decree, "a new creature", made unconquerable by his holy strength.[16a]

All this is made clear to the people in the Song of the King, in which he proclaims his election on the enthronement festival. He has received a divine oracle (probably through incubation the night before the festival, cf. 1 Kings 3: 3ff.),[17] which he now proclaims to the people.[18] The Psalm is phenomenologically a parallel and type of the Christmas Gospel: The Saviour has been born! Isaiah 9: 1–6 belongs to the same literary type. This is, moreover, significant not only for religious phenomenology, but also for Christian theology.

The Psalm gives the following description of its own situation. First, we get a description of the revolt of the "kings of the earth", an historification of the mythical powers of the Chaos. Then follows the reaction of God, who not only laughs his enemies to scorn, but also speaks a fearfully threatening word to them. To this is added to his Son, the king, the promise that he is to be ruler of the world. And, finally, the king warns the enemies that they must surrender before the divine wrath consumes them. We shall see that this pattern of the poem returns in later periods and determines "the Messianic situation".[19]

# 3

## THE PSALMS IN THE RITUAL

Now that we have sketched the pattern of Psalm 2, we shall find it interesting to attempt a determination of its place in the ritual.

One might think that this question cannot be answered at all. The ritual of the Enthronement Festival is not described in detail anywhere in the Old Testament, and the "ritual pattern" of the Near East is nowhere found in its complete form. It is, in fact, an admittedly hypothetical reconstruction. What we have is not one "pattern", but several related "patterns", with many similarities, but also with important differences.[1] The concrete examples of "patterns" are hardly ever complete, but we possess material which is satisfactory enough to enable us to set forth some fairly well-founded generalizations.

The method by which we can supplement the concrete forms of the ritual is the usual so-called "form-critical" method applied by Gunkel and his followers. It was used by Mowinckel in his successful attempt to describe the Enthronement Festival, and it has never been seriously challenged. As long as this is the case, the basis of the "ritual pattern" of Mowinckel, for example, cannot be seriously disputed.[2] The main principle is that the poems themselves furnish the evidence by which their "setting in life" may be determined. This is only an application of a common philological method which has been used for ages, but generally only to determine the "place in time" of a text by means of its assumed historical allusions. It surely cannot be called illegitimate to apply the same method to other features in literary productions, especially in the Ancient East, where forms and styles are strictly developed to fit special situations. And here the comparative method is also of importance. For when we find poems outside Israel, which formally and stylistically (to the minutest details) resemble poems in the

Old Testament (the only difference being that the non-Israelite poems, e.g. in Babylonia, are furnished with rubrics, determining their cultic use), we are entitled to surmise that the Israelite poems are of the same kind, and we are obliged to use the hints they contain to help us determine their function.

This is no "metasemasiological" method, as Ginsberg insinuates.[3] It is merely an application of sound philological principles according to Oriental literary conditions.[4] Therefore, we do not consider that it is a hopeless task to aim at a reconstruction of the broad outlines of Israelite ritual. It has been done admirably by Mowinckel in his *Psalmenstudien*, and (as Frankfort admits) by Hans Schmidt in his *Die Thronfahrt Jahves am Fest der Jahreswende* (1927). For our purpose, we may begin by referring to a beautiful example of this kind of reconstruction—the article of L. Dürr on Psalm 110 in relation to recent investigations of the Ancient Oriental cults.[5] Mowinckel in his *Psalmenstudien* gave only a brief treatment of Psalm 2 and Psalm 110 as "oracles belonging to the liturgy of the day of anointing the king", described as "*agendarisch vorgeschriebene Stücke der Salbungsliturgie*".[6] Dürr referred to the fact that we possess ancient Oriental sources allowing us to follow in detail the ritual of the enthronement of kings. We know the Assyrian liturgy,[7] which among other interesting features contains the fact that the Supreme Eunuchs must kiss the feet of the king twice (cf. Psalm 2: 11–12). From Babylon, we know the ceremony of "taking the hands of the God" by the king in the ritual of the New Year Festival. In Egypt, we find the ritual of the Sed-Festival, the jubilee festival of the king; and the so-called "dramatic papyrus of the Ramesseum", in its "play at the enthronement of the king", furnishes us with knowledge concerning the actual cultic acts on that occasion.[8]

The great measure of agreement between the rites of the different Oriental cultural provinces (including Hittite and the Ugaritic examples) led British and American scholars to develop their theory of a "ritual pattern" common to the Ancient East. This material was reviewed afresh and investigated in a most stimulating and independent manner by Ivan Engnell in his *Studies in Divine Kingship* (1943).

Dürr said in his work on Psalm 110 that this poem is for the

Israelite area what the Ramesseum Papyrus is for Egypt. He thinks that the different acts of the coronation festival stand out distinctly behind the psalm. The psalm gives the text accompanying the rites,[9] and so we can in fact speak of a coronation ritual, or an agenda for the ceremonies, which were accompanied by the words of the prophet speaking the oracle of Psalm 110. Dürr finds in the psalm the Enthronement (v. 1), the Investiture (v. 2), especially with the sceptre, the Acclamation (v. 3), the Ordination as priest (v. 4), the Promise of victory over enemies (vv. 5–6), and the sacramental cup of water from the Holy Well (v. 7).

What is missing from Dürr's presentation is the idea that this ritual is connected with the New Year Festival and its Creation drama. The fact that Dürr does not find the feature of the proclamation of the king as "Son of God" in v. 3 is easily explained by his retention of the traditional, corrupt text.[10] It has also to be remembered that the Ras Shamra material had not yet been published when Dürr wrote his article. He keeps the common "political" interpretation of the enemies, which, as we noted above, are an "historification" of the enemies of God in the Creation myth.

In making an attempt to reconstruct the main lines of the ritual, we shall, first and foremost, use the Israelite material.[11] We shall take our starting point in the Old Testament Psalms and from a combination of the undoubtedly Royal Psalms see whether a tolerably coherent picture will emerge. Whether such a picture could reproduce the right succession of the different acts of the ritual, we cannot say with absolute certainty. Upon the whole, the pattern described by Dürr is likely to be confirmed.

I may note in passing that I cannot see that the "pattern" proposed by Hooke[12] is so evidently wrong, as Frankfort says. There are many variations. Frankfort especially emphasizes the human character of the Mesopotamian king, as opposed to the absolute godhead of Pharaoh. As I have said elsewhere,[13] there is a truth in the stress he places on these different attitudes. The difference is a parallel to the much later difference between "monophysitism" and "Nestorianism", the latter stressing the gulf between men and God, and the former obliterating it. But in some cases, the gulf is also overcome in Mesopotamia.[14]

We can, therefore, make Dürr's description our starting point, supplemented by what we have said already above about the essential cultic interpretation of the Psalms.

At the centre stands the *ritual combat*. The victory of God and his Anointed over their antagonists, who attempt to prevent the good work of Creation; the preparations for battle; the battle itself; and combined with the battle the suffering of the king and the god under the heavy attacks of the enemies (which in the non-Israelite rites culminate in the death of the god);[15] his salvation and return from the underworld; his final seizing of power and his enthronement in the newly-built temple—these elements make up the main content of the festival. Consequently, the most important thing that we shall be able to say about the arrangement of the psalms in the ritual will be how they are related to the central theme, the ritual combat—whether, that is, a certain psalm belongs to a point before, in, or after the battle. Here, *Psalm 2* is again important. It is quite obvious that this poem must be placed *before* the combat. The contents are decisive in this respect. The Psalm says that God is certain that the victory will be His and that of His Anointed, even before the fight has begun against the conspiracy of the enemies. The poem concludes with a threatening warning to them to change their minds. The oracle is, as was said above, God's ultimatum to them *before* the beginning of the combat.

*Psalm 110* must be placed in a similar situation. This poem, too, is an oracle promising the king what he needs before entering the battle against the enemies, whom he will be able to annihilate by the mighty help of his God. Even the drink from the Holy Well must be meant for the strengthening of the hero before the fight.[16] The parallel sentence in the Ugaritic text I D 152, which says that "the king fasts and goes to the fountain", appears to be a preparation for the execrations which Dan'el hurls at the murderers of his son. On the assumption that Dürr's interpretation of *Psalm 110* is right, we must take it that enthronement, investiture, proclamation of the divine sonship of the king and of his priesthood, as well as sacramental communion, are placed *before* the ritual combat, as a preparation for it. The last verse of *Psalm 110* must not be regarded as an insignificant remnant of a larger section. On the contrary, this verse is the culmination of the psalm. The communion, the drink of the Fountain of Life, is the mighty strengthening of the elect warrior, who will fight the divine battle against the devils of the Chaos and help to re-create the world.

If *Psalm 20* should have its "setting in life" in the coronation ritual, it would also belong to the rites *before* the fight. Even if this psalm proved to be a liturgy for a special situation before an actual war, this would not alter the interpretation very much; because such a special situation would always be an actualization of the ritual combat of the coronation rite.[17] The same is the case with *Psalm 21*.

On the other hand, the *Royal Psalms of Lamentation* must be regarded as accompanying the ritual combat itself.[18] When the theory is accepted that most psalms (at least in their formal origin) must be derived from the royal ritual, we can naturally draw upon much more material than the comparatively few psalms which expressly describe themselves as Royal Psalms. I should count, for example, Psalms 3, 11, 12, 13 and 14 among the Psalms which describe the Suffering Innocent, although I must make the reservation that a number of such psalms may be explained by Hans Schmidt's theory that they are "prayers of persons accused of crimes".[19] In addition, I reckon *Psalms 22, 69* and *27* with the Royal Psalms.[20] Here we encounter the "adoption theme" from Psalm 2 in the form of the king's being "taken up" (27: 10; cf. 22: 10)[21] by Yahweh. *Psalm 28* describes itself as a Royal Psalm (v. 8). That *Psalm 42–43* is the lament of a leading person in the congregation is generally agreed (42:4?) and it may be associated with the fight against the powers of Chaos, during which the sufferer has been overcome by the enemies and is passing through the waters of the nether world on the way to the land of death.[22] *Psalm 52* can be understood as a speech repudiating the enemies before the battle[23] (cf. the conclusion of Psalm 2). The same is the case with *Psalms 54* and *55*, perhaps also with *57, 58* and *59*. I shall not investigate all the psalms; for further material, the reader may refer to ch. III of my Danish book,

*Det sakrale kongedömme.* Instead, I wish to examine a special theme of the *Psalms of Lamentation.*[24]

In his review of Engell's *Studies on Divine Kingship* and Widengren's article *Det sakrala kungadömet bland öst-och väst-semiter,* Mowinckel[25] emphasized his objection that we have no proof that the king was regarded as being *really* dead and resuscitated. Mowinckel holds that even if the gods were thought of as dying and rising again, it is not certain that this was true of the *king.*[26] The fact that the Babylonian king is described as penitent, in the well known scene in the New Year Festival, where his royal insignia are taken away and he is boxed on the ears and pulled by the ears by the priest, does not mean that he *dies.* An identification of death and penitence is not found in any text. The king can "experience" the death of the god, as the mystics speak of experiencing and becoming "one" with God; but, like the mystics, the king does not "really" die. This, according to Mowinckel, is important for the understanding of Isaiah 53, where the Servant of Yahweh "really" dies.[27] Mowinckel says that when the person praying in the Psalms (in many cases the king), is described as dead, as being on the way to the underworld, the expression is not meant literally.[28] The king "has got death in himself", the realm of Death has seized him by its claws, but the person praying always asks for his liberation, lest the realm of Death should get him into its power. The Old Testament Psalms generally pray for salvation from death, that it may not be too late; they do not pray for the resurrection of the sufferer. Widengren can find in the Babylonian material only the fact that the king is killed "symbolically"—through the "vicarious" death of a black bull. But that is "experienced", not "real" death.

In a later paper,[29] Widengren published new material concerning this problem. He attempts to prove that *Psalm 88*: 2–9 is full of themes which are connected with the death of Tammuz. He does not take the view that *Psalm 88* is the original cultic text, which was recited by the king at the point of the ritual when he is "mythically" in the underworld. There can be no doubt that Widengren has collected in this paper a long series of parallel expressions from ancient Sumerian texts which are very important for the mode of expression found in the psalm. Further, he has pointed out expressions in other psalms which deal with resurrection and may be understood as witnessing to the ideas of Israelite popular religion, influenced, as it was, by Canaanite beliefs (Psalm 35: 23; 44: 24; 59: 5: "Wake up!" Psalm 18: 47: "Yahweh lives!"). The latter expression, which is generally used as an oath, is taken by Widengren to have been originally a cultic word, proclaiming the resurrection of the god. Here, therefore, it would seem possible to trace a conception of God as dying and rising again in Israelite religion (or, more precisely, in Israelite *popular* religion).[30] This may be the case.[31] But then Widengren continues: "This is what we must expect, because the rôle of the king in the cult as suffering and being in the hands of the underworld, but also as victor and coming forth in living power, would be unexplained without this supposition". As far as I can see, this is just the point which needs to be proved, namely, that the king is described as *really* dead and risen. The opposite view of Mowinckel is at all events not refuted, namely, that the king "experiences" the death of the god, without *"really"* dying himself.[32] The text of Psalm 88 does not speak of "real" death. In vv. 3–5, the Sufferer is not *in* the land of the Dead, but *near* to it. He is not dead, but is looked upon *as* dead. Even if we accept the rule that in the ancient cultures similarity is tantamount to identification,[33] we cannot conclude that in these verses the Sufferer is, in reality, dead. This position cannot be disposed of by calling it a result of "logicism". Even v. 5 must be modified by this context. The Sufferer in Psalm 88 is not yet dead. He fears death and anticipates its terrors, as Mowinckel says. There is no talk of "real" death.

In this connection, I come to *Psalm 18* and the exclamation "Yahweh lives!"[34] As was suggested above, it is possible that this was an ancient cultic exclamation, a "Christ is risen!" of the ancient popular religion of Canaan and of "Canaanistic" circles in Israel. This is, of course, very interesting; but does it say anything of the Old Testament Royal Psalm and its conception of God? In Psalm 18, too, the king is saved from Sheol, before it is too late. Yahweh descends with tremendous force into the underworld and seizes the king, just before

Death overcomes him finally. The cry "Yahweh lives!" does not mean that Yahweh has been dead and has risen again. On the contrary, here the victorious vitality of God is celebrated, His "immortality", His power which intervenes and saves, without dying. The exclamation is a concise expression of that feature which Johs. Pedersen has emphasized as characterizing genuine Israelite religion in opposition to Canaanite cult and Canaanitish-Israelite syncretism.[35] Similar observations may be made about the cry, "Wake up!"[36]

It must be admitted, however, that there are texts with expressions of a kind which apparently imply the "real" death of the Sufferer. This is true of *Psalm 30*, which is very similar to Psalm 88. Here, God (v. 2) has "drawn up" the Sufferer, and the Hebrew root employed (*dlh*) associates the act of God with the act of drawing water from a well in a bucket (*deli*). This imagery must be understood against the background of the conception of Sheol in the likeness of a cistern[37] and, therefore, it points to the complex of conceptions surrounding the underworld. There is a correspondence to this picture in v. 3 where God has made the Sufferer "ascend from Sheol" and "revived" him. But the psalm is placed in the mouth of a man singing to the people, and there is no analogy in the Book of Psalms which allows us to ascribe this psalm to someone who has been "really" resuscitated from death. In addition to the phrases just alluded to, there are others (as in Ps. 88) which do not presuppose the "real" death of the Sufferer, but even signify that he has *not* been "really" dead. The poet must have imagined the person praying in the psalm as being a concrete living person. Is it possible that he was thought to be "really" dead, when we are told that he "called out" to Yahweh, "made supplication" to him, and was "healed"? V. 10, too, must presuppose that he has not been "really" dead. I know, of course, that the ancient peoples considered the threat of death as good as death itself;[38] but that is precisely what Mowinckel says in opposition to Engnell and Widengren. When we interpret the psalms, we must presuppose that the Sufferers are not "really" dead, and that they were not conceived of as such by the Ancients.

In the Old Testament, there is never any thought of the

"real" death of the king. Mowinckel's thesis concerning the difference between the descriptions of "death" in the psalms and that of Isaiah 53 is in the main correct.[39] The king in the psalms is described as being in extremely dangerous situations. When the enemies of the Sufferer in *Psalm 22* are described as animals, they are probably meant to be demons.[40] This may also connect it with the descriptions of the fight of the king against his enemies: he has been captured and tortured by the powers of the underworld. They are expressly mentioned in the conclusion of the song (v. 30).[41, 42]

A Royal Psalm of Lamentation, which must be mentioned in this connection because of the special problems it raises, is the great *Psalm 89*. That this elaborate liturgical composition[43] presents the same ideas of the sacral king as the other Royal Psalms is evident. We find the notion of the king as "Son of God" expressed by the king himself in vv. 27–28. The king appeals to the ritual Word of God from Psalms 2:7 and 110:3. In the preceding part of the liturgy, Yahweh speaks of the victory over the enemies of God and His King. The promise of world dominion (cf. Psalm 2:8) is expressed here in v. 26, where it is said that the king has dominion over "the sea", i.e. that he shares the victorious results of the creative combat.

The position of this liturgy in the coronation ritual is, however, not quite clear; and this may have consequences for some of the other psalms mentioned above. We have said that it is not certain that all the royal psalms of lamentation belong to the coronation rites, and so we must examine the subject a little further.

*Psalm 89* has, it is true, been connected with the ritual of the coronation.[44] An attempt has been made to find some "Tammuz-themes" in it, e.g. the king has lost crown and throne. This is certainly mentioned in vv. 40 and 45. But it may be felt that the description of the suffering of the king (vv. 39–46) is of a more "historical" kind than in, for example, Psalm 22. Here, the enemies are not only "the nations", but "the neighbours", "those who pass by". We get a more vivid picture of a "real" war than in Psalm 22.

When, however, we remember the discussions concerning the interpretation of the KRT-Legend from Ras Shamra, we recognize that we must be cautious in this respect. The KRT-Texts were at first interpreted as "historical" texts. But Johs. Pedersen and Engnell have proved them to be ritual texts.[45] As far as I can see, Johs. Pedersen, after the later treatment by Engnell, will have to modify his opinions a little.[46] The KRT-Texts either seem to belong to a special wedding-rite of the king, or the wedding of the king is regarded as part of the enthronement festival and the *hieros gamos* rites.[47] It may be a "bye-text" of the great coronation ritual. However that may be, the KRT-Texts are at all events not "historical" in the narrow sense of the word. They are in some way or another connected with a ritual. And the same may perhaps be said of *Psalm 89*. What here look like the remnants of an "historical" situation of distress could be a strongly "historified" description of the ritual combat from the Creation drama; and then the psalm would be a parallel to Psalm 22. In both psalms, God is accused of unfaithfulness. He has not intervened on the side of his Anointed according to his promise in the coronation oracles (Psalms 2 and 110). In such compositions, we experience something of the immense excitement of the cultic drama, the fear with which the worshippers (and above all the king) must have lived through the rites—a desperate fear like that of the Day of the Passion, before the Easter experience of the apostles changed everything into a conviction of victory.

On the view that a concrete occasion of distress is the background of *Psalm 89*, we might explain the situation of the liturgy as that of a service held during a time of defeat in war. (I should still interpret Psalm 60 in this way.) The "historistic" interpretation of *Psalm 89* referred it to the death of Josiah after the battle of Megiddo in 609. Assuming the cult-dramatic interpretation of the Psalms, we should then say that the liturgy for special occasions was influenced by the great enthronement festival. But it is not difficult to see that this distinction rests upon an illusion.[48] A special liturgy of lamentation on the occasion of a military defeat would simply be a scene from the enthronement festival, that is, the scene of the drama which represents the passion of the king in the ritual combat. The special service would appear as an "actualization" of the New Year celebrations and their inherent "mythical" ideas. The question raised above, as to whether Royal Psalms of Lamentation were composed for the enthronement festival or for services on special concrete occasions, must accordingly be abandoned as relatively unimportant. Even if the psalms were not written for the annual New Year festival,[49] but for other situations in the life of the king, e.g. illness,[50] and even if we have to reckon with the fact that the Israelite-Jewish Psalms, which must be regarded as relatively "late" literature,[51] have been to a great extent "democratized",[52] nevertheless, we must acknowledge that their formal language is still stamped by the "original" situation of the royal ritual, and that they are, therefore, important for our knowledge of the Enthronement Festival of Yahweh and His Anointed.

According to what has been said above, it is comparatively easy to give a rough sketch of the position of the Psalms in the ritual. The detail we must leave to Engnell, who still owes us the second part of his *Studies in Divine Kingship*.[53] I would like, however, to say something about the great liturgy of *Psalm 132*.[54]

It would, in my opinion, be justifiable to call this composition a Liturgy of the Entry of the Ark of Yahweh. The king is, however, so dominating a figure, that it would perhaps be more appropriate to speak of it as a liturgy for a royal jubilee, or for the annual festival of the enthronement.[55] The ritual found in the composition is strongly reminiscent of the Babylonian New Year celebrations on the 5th Nisan, when the king is treated as a penitent.[56] The most interesting feature in this psalm, however, is the rôle played by Israelite tradition, as represented by the Ark of the Covenant. The sufferings of the king, named in the beginning of the composition, and invoked as the merits of David, do not concern his *descensus ad inferos*, but his interest in the lost palladium of Israel, the Holy Ark. It means that David has sacrificed his own comfort in the service of his God. For the idea is that Yahweh has disappeared with his "dwelling place" (v. 7), "his footstool" (*ibid.*). The great deed of David seems to have been to save the god. The theme of the descensus-psalms appears to have been inverted: the king must rescue the god! That this thought was not quite alien to Israel is seen in Judges 5: 23*b*, where a town is cursed because it did not "come to the help of the Lord". It also agrees with the conception associated with the Patriarchs in the ancient legends, where, e.g. Jacob is described as being stronger than God (Genesis 32: 23ff.). The stories of the adventures of the Ark among the Philistines in 1 Samuel 4–6[57] must be connected with 2 Samuel 6 as reflections of ritual celebrations in the temple.[58] The chapters in 1 Samuel prove that the idea is not simply that David saves Yahweh. Yahweh has fought the decisive part of the battle by his mighty signs and portents against the Philistines and their god Dagon, by which he has delivered himself from captivity. The story appears to be an "historification" of the "myth of the fight of the gods" on Yahwistic soil, developed under the influence of the wars of liberation against the Philistines under David. History here has re-interpreted the rituals—as at the Red Sea under Moses.[59] As an "historification", the story is an interesting phenomenological parallel inside the Old Testament to the legend of the Exodus, to which it expressly refers (1 Samuel 4: 8). The Philistines have replaced the Egyptians.

*Psalm 132* belongs to a ritual related to this "historified myth". Yahweh returns from the "Hell" of the Land of the Philistines, where he has defeated his enemy Dagon. In the last phase of the fight David has come to his help and has brought him into his sanctuary. David here plays the rôle of the forerunner preparing the way of Yahweh, just as the Messiah does in Malachi 3: 1ff. *Psalm 132*, therefore, must be the conclusion and the culmination of the ritual, parallel to *Psalm 24*, where Yahweh returns to his sanctuary as the "King of Glory". The story of the Ark is a "Davidic version" of the myth, and this is to be understood as the background of the Patriarchal position given to David in Chronicles, where he is described as the founder of the cult in Zion. The festival instituted by David was imitated later by Jeroboam I in Bethel and Dan (1 Kings 12: 32). But the important fact for us to notice is that in this version of the "pattern" also, the death of the god is excluded. What we have said above concerning this theme,[60] here gets a most probable confirmation. Here, Yahweh's *descensus ad inferos* is not to be regarded as death, but as victorious battle. In the land of death, "historified" as the land of the Philistines, he has played according to his own will and pleasure with Dagon and his worshippers and made them utterly ridiculous. The humorous element in the legends of 1 Samuel 5–6 must not be overlooked! The enemies were forced to arrange his return to his own land—"Death could not control him"[61] (Acts 2: 24). This word from the New Testament, used of the Messiah, could be used in the Old Covenant of Yahweh Himself, as we see in the story of the Ark.

The mighty deeds of David in this connection are now (according to *Psalm 132*) the basis of the prayer for the dynasty. The Patriarch of the Royal House has "come to the help of Yahweh". With reference to this meritorious act, the liturgy prays for his successor, and the divine promise to David is repeated in conditional forms. In addition, the blessing is pronounced over the Sanctuary, for the election of the Sanctuary is the ground of the divine promise to David (vv. 13ff.). In all the latter features, a priestly tendency to subordinate the kingdom to the priesthood reveals itself. This is paralleled in the Babylonian ritual, where the king receives his royal insignia from the hands of the priest.

It is of interest to note that *Psalm 132* appears to be a special Jerusalemitic-Davidic form of the ritual. The festival instituted by David seems to be a creation with an historical root, especially marked by the policy of David.[62] From the Davidic war of liberation, the Enthronement Festival acquired (at least for a time) a "new myth", an "actualization" of the Exodus-legend, which it threatened to supersede.[63] But it is significant that David apparently did not aim at a change of this kind. The genuine Israelite tradition must have been so firmly attached to the Passover-celebrations that he did not venture to interfere with this festival. According to 1 Kings 12: 32, David's festival was celebrated in the eighth month, i.e. in the autumn, like the New Year festival known to us from the laws. David's festival seems to have been one of the elements which served to "Israelitize" the Canaanite winegathering festival, which developed into the Israelite Feast of Booths.

Leaving the position of the Psalms in Ritual with this brief

c

treatment, we turn now to a question which will be of import-
ance for the following investigations, and for the theological
interpretation of the Psalms. The question is: How far can the
Psalms be regarded as "Messianic"? or (what amounts to the
same question) Can the Israelite king be called "Messiah"?
In the rest of this book, we shall attempt to draw a line leading
from the ancient Sacral Kingship, as it is described in the
Psalms, through the Songs of the Suffering Servant in Deutero-
Isaiah, to the "Son of Man" of later Judaism and the New
Testament. What has been said in this chapter is intended only
as a brief and sketchy supplement to the preceding sections, in
order to make it clear that *Psalm 2* does not stand alone in
cultic poetry, but is organically bound up with other Royal
Psalms, forming a "pattern" which, through significant
changes, emerges as a feature of the first importance in the
New Testament and the christological doctrine of the Church.

# 4

## THE KING AS THE PRESENT MESSIAH

*Can the Word "Messianic" be used of the King of Israel?*

WHEN we put this question as the sub-title to the chapter, we do not intend to return to the interpretation of the primitive Church, where it was held that the Psalms witness directly to Jesus as the Christ. Neither Psalm 2 nor 110 is concerned with Jesus. The warlike figure, breaking the heads of his enemies like the gigantic Pharaoh on Egyptian wall-pictures, has, directly, nothing to do with the crucified Mediator of the New Testament. Indirectly, a connection can be established; but this will not become apparent until we have finished the rapid survey which we intend to give in this book. The king of the Psalms is the victor over Death, like Christ of the New Testament, but between the two several important changes in the figure of the Messiah take place. The king in Psalms 2 and 110 and in the Psalms of the Righteous Sufferer, in short, the king of the Enthronement Festival, is a type, a prefiguration of the New Testament Christ. But the Psalms do not deal directly with Jesus.

Our question is one concerning a definition. What must we understand by "Messiah"?

Scientific literature on this subject in recent years has no clear terminology. For example, Graham and May[1] speak of the kings in the Ancient East in the second millennium B.C. as "Messianic": "They stood as incarnations and symbols of the fructifying, protecting, and healing powers of the consort of the mother-goddess"; and they declare, "In whatever particulars it may differ from the earlier messianism, that which is reflected so prominently in the Old Testament is a lineal descendant from it". Further, they refer to Breasted,[2] who traces the origins of Messianism back to Egypt.

Engnell and Widengren do not agree completely on this question. Engnell says,[3] "By 'messianism' I mean elaborate king ideology, not 'eschatological' messianism". This view he has later[4] explained in detail: "Sacral or divine kingship is the accepted term for an institution, simultaneously of a religious and political kind, found in a majority of different cultural areas, and meaning that the king 'by the Grace of God' in his own person incarnates the god and in the cult plays the part of the god. At the same time, however, he also represents, in a special manner, the Collective, the Whole, the People, and so stands between man and god as the Mediator on whom everything and everybody depends. On him depend victory and well-being, rain and fertility, nay the entire integrity of Nature and Human Life, the natural order of the cosmos, which he maintains against the Chaos Powers above all through his cultic functions. In the ideology connected with his person these relations are reflected. And when they are cultivated into such a degree of purity that the king stands as an ideal figure with expectations of salvation bound up with him, then we already have reached a state about which the term 'Messianism' must be used—a term which accordingly need not necessarily have an eschatological aspect."

This definition has, as far as we can see, disarmed the criticism of Widengren.[5] Widengren wanted the first short definition of Engnell to be widened, stressing the state of the king as Saviour, Son of God and as the "Envoy" ("Apostle") of God, as Incarnation of the Cosmic Law. These conceptions are included (at least to a great extent) in the more elaborate definition of Engnell just quoted.

Against this definition, Mowinckel and others have voiced a rather strong opposition.[6] They have emphasized that in order to have a clear conception of what is meant by "Messiah" and "Messianic", we must have a clear definition, and that this is only possible if we use the words with a clear "eschatological" meaning. Mowinckel says that "whoever says 'Messiah' also says 'Eschatology'; and an ancient Oriental Eschatology as Gressmann and Sellin imagined has never existed".

In this discussion, I have taken sides with Engnell and Widengren. The question is mainly a terminological issue. The word "Messianic" in popular as well as scientific speech commonly carries an "eschatological" meaning. The words "eschatology" and "eschatological", on the other hand, are not always clearly defined. About thirty years ago, Hölscher tried to clear up the matter. He defined the terms as denoting the great drama at the absolute end of the world and the beginning of a new one, and claimed that they should be used exclusively of the period treated under the heading "Eschatology" by Christian Dogmatics—"*De Novissimis*".[7]

It must, however, be acknowledged that the difference between the "cultic" and the "eschatological" interpretations of the Enthronement Psalms is not very great. The characteristic feature of the cultic interpretation is that Salvation—at all events in principle—is an actual fact of the present day. "*Consummatum est!*" could very well be the concluding words of the ritual combat of the Creation Play, with the sufferings and the victory of the Divine King. Creation is Salvation which is repeated in the ritual. Salvation is a possession, but it must be won again every year. That is the meaning of the Ritual. The fact of Creation is fundamental for the assurance that the world stands secure, is in steady equilibrium through the victory over the Dragon, the Powers of Evil, the Sea, the Nations, Sin, Death, and the Devil. The Preacher of this victory is the king. He has personally fought on the side of his God, has given Yahweh's oracle that victory is certain. In the lamentations of the Creation Ritual, he himself suffers the excitement of the combat and prays with his people for the victory of their God. In the corresponding Psalms of Thanksgiving, he praises God for the fulfilment. The Psalms experience in living actuality what Eschatology expects. Therefore, the king of the Psalms and of Eschatology is in the main the same;[8] they are both bearers of Salvation. That some people want to restrict the word "Messiah" to the Saviour of Eschatology is based only on a praiseworthy desire for clarity of expression.

When we know what we mean, and are sure that we shall not be misunderstood by readers and listeners,[9] it will be much more in tune with the material which we have to investigate and describe to use the expressions "Messiah" and "Messianic" of a figure which changes through the ages, but still retains certain essential characteristic features even through changed circumstances. The words may very appropriately be used of

the pre-exilic Israelite sacral king and even of the ancient
Oriental divine king; they may also be used of his "lineal
descendant", the eschatological Son of David of later Judaism
and equally of the Son of Man. We shall be able to see how
the Early Church utilized the ancient material to build up its
dogmas of the Trinity and Christology. This change, this
*Gestaltwandlung*, took place through the catastrophes of Israelite
and Jewish history, which made the assurance of the ancient
days unsafe and converted it into expectation—the belief that
the fulfilment would come in the future. The connection with
the cultic calendar was severed. Under the influence of the
religion of Israel with its strongly historical orientation, the
ancient Oriental conception of life as a circle was broken. The
circle—with its constant repetitions of the same events—was
replaced by the straight line of History, at the end of which
the New Creation is expected and hoped for. The New Creation is described by means of elements drawn from the ancient
Enthronement Festival. To use Mowinckel's words from
*Psalmenstudien II*, Israel made its way "from experience to
hope". The Saviour, the Divine King of Eschatology, is, however, phenomenologically the same figure as the Davidic sacral
king, the Son of God—even *'elôhîm* (Psalm 45: 7).[10] Both may
therefore be called "Messiah", corresponding to the title used
of the king by pre-exilic literature (e.g. 1 and 2 Samuel and
Psalm 2: 6), "the Anointed of Yahweh".

If, then, we can describe the pre-exilic and the ancient
Oriental king as a "Messianic" type, we must now add that
the conception of "primeval" or "primordial" Man is also an
important component of the picture.[11]

# 5

## MESSIAH AND "FIRST MAN"

In a comprehensive study,[1] Mowinckel has told us how he explains the origin of the notion "Son of Man" in the Gospels, the Ethiopic Enoch and the Ezra-Apocalypse. In his view, the idea of the Son of Man in the Gospels was not derived exegetically from Daniel 7, nor has the idea anything to do with the conception of the "Messianic" kings of the Old Testament. The Messiah was never clothed with Divinity in the absolute metaphysical sense, as was the *"Urmensch"*, the "Primeval Man" of the numerous *"Anthropos"* and *"Urmensch"* myths of Ancient Oriental lands, of later Judaism, Mandaeism, Manichaeism, in short, of the entire world of Gnosticism. These ideas are supposed to have their roots in myths from Babylonia, Iran and India. The Old Testament Messiah has nothing to do with Paradise. The connection of the ideas of Paradise with the "Messiah" of the Book of Isaiah (9: 1–6; 11: 1–10) is said to be a "secondary" feature. The Old Testament Messiah has nothing to do with doctrines of world periods. He comes *in* history, called by the God of history, not at the end of history and of time, between the aeons.

This last claim seems to be right. The Messiah of pre-exilic days (Mowinckel, of course, will not speak of him as "Messiah") is not an "eschatological" figure, when "Eschatology" is understood in the manner of Hölscher and Mowinckel. It is also right to say that the Son of Man of later literature is much more "metaphysical", much more "transcendent", than the Old Testament "Messiah" in Isaiah 9, 11, and Micah 5. But that this "Messiah" is both Man and God, is nevertheless obvious. How he has attained this status we were not told. Isaiah 7 preserves the idea of the royal prince as being born of the queen-goddess, and the same is possibly the case in the corrupt passage Psalm 110: 3, according to the evidence of the more intelligible traditions in the LXX and the Vulgate. Psalm 2 expressly uses the idea of adoption. Both these passages referring to the king of Israel, the "present Messiah", and those referring to the coming king, whom we might call the "Son of David", therefore describe their object as in some sense Divine; cf. Psalm 45: 7 (the present "Messiah"). In Isaiah 9: 6, the future king is called "Mighty God" and Micah 5: 4 also places him in a relationship to Yahweh[2] which is that of a man elevated above normal humanity. The ideas of Paradise in Isaiah 11 are so organically connected with the context that nothing can justify their being regarded as "secondary". If the promises in Isaiah 9 and 11 and Micah 5 were found in the Book of Psalms, nobody could object to their being classed with the kind of Royal Psalms represented, e.g. by Psalm 72, where ideas of an earthly Paradise are connected with the "present Messiah", the king of Israel. The lack of "transcendence" and "metaphysical" features is due to the earlier age, when "dualism" and "transcendence" have not yet created a real "eschatology", of which these features are characteristic.

The fact that there is no idea of world periods in the earlier texts is also probably a consequence of their different date. Teaching about world periods belongs to a time later than the "Messianic" texts of *circa* 600. The "Messiah" of this period is an earlier form of the idea and accordingly it differs from later developments of the figure. But the "Messiah" of the texts from Isaiah and Micah is, nevertheless, a figure with features of divinity and sacral kingship. If a conjecture is permissible, the divinity of the king might even be found in Micah 5: 1. In the second line of the verse LXX[A] reads *hegoùmenos* after the verb *jêṣê'*. Mowinckel in his commentary in the Norwegian annotated translation, therefore, reads *melek*. But it would be better to assume a double haplography and read *'êl*, "god", "a god" (cf. *'êl gibbôr* in Isaiah 9: 5). The letters 'aleph and lamed have disappeared between the 'aleph in *jêṣê'* and the lamed in *lihᵉjôt*. This could be explained, too, by the anti-Canaanite reaction and the tendency of later Judaism to avoid the use of divine terms for kings. And the same tendency could account for the reading of the LXX. However, even if we do not pay any attention to such conjectural possibilities, we may note that it is most probable that the ancient promises of the books of Isaiah 1–39 and Micah describe the coming king as the newly-born miraculous being, the divine Saviour and the king of Paradise.

The latter feature belongs to the complex of ideas in the Creation Legends. We find the description of the "First Man" as ruler over the animals in Genesis 1 and 2, that is, both in the "Priestly" and the "Yahwistic" tradition of the Creation Legend (Genesis 1: 28 and 2: 19–20). It is at least possible—even probable—that Psalm 8, which is so strongly dependent upon Genesis 1 or the material preserved there, connects the same ideas with the First Man. When Mowinckel[3] finds both in Genesis 1 and Psalm 8 only allusions to "men" in general, I cannot follow him. In both texts, we have descriptions of "Man" as ruler over all living creatures. Mowinckel and Sjöberg do not see that the distinction between "Man" and "Men" in such a case is not applicable to Israelite texts. The Genesis text speaks of the Patriarch of the Human Race, who is to "rule" the world, i.e. to be king. "First Man" is described here as "First King". Moreover, I cannot find any justification for denying that the parallel text in Psalm 8 means the same thing.[4] In my opinion, both Genesis 1 and Psalm 8 speak of "First Man" and "First King". In Psalm 8 this "First Man" (who, by the way, is called "Son of Man") is also "but little lower than God"—a characteristic Israelite devaluation of the Oriental "divine kingship", but, nevertheless, an important piece of evidence that ideas of Divine Kingship have left their mark on Israelite texts.

On the other hand, in Isaiah 9 and 11 and Micah 5 the divine, or nearly divine, sacral-king is not described as "First Man". But since "First King" and "First Man" are identical in Genesis 1 and Psalm 8, where the Patriarch of the human race and the race of kings are described, it would seem justifiable to hold that this idea must be implied, e.g. in Micah 5, where the king is also associated with "days of old", the Primeval Age. We have found it probable that the "then" (*'âz*) in Psalm 2 alludes to the election of the king, the Son of God, at the time of creation. His "birth" or "adoption" as

"Son of God" in Psalm 2 is the ritual "repetition" or "actualization" of the primordial institution of king and kingship. What happened then to the Patriarch of Kings and Men happens again to the actual "King" and "Man" in the Coronation Rite. Psalm 8 contains the same identification of "Man" and "King". The "Son of Man" in 8: 5ff. is king, "nearly a god" (5), "crowned" (5), ruler of the world (6) and of the animals (7ff.). And, as we have said, the connections between the Psalm and Genesis 1 prove the same. Accordingly, this "Son of Man" is "First Man" and "First King". He is, of course, also "Man in General",[5] for these two must not be severed from one another as we individualistic Westerners suppose. Sjöberg does go so far as to acknowledge *reminiscences* of a description of the primordial king in Genesis 1 and Psalm 8, but he also attempts to retain the distinction just mentioned between the primordial king and "men in general". He points out that the verb "rule" in Genesis 1: 28 is plural. In my view, this plural does not indicate "men in general", but the fact that the context speaks of the "First Couple", i.e. the first *hieros gamos*. And at all events, as Psalm 8 does not use the plural of the verb, the inference from the plural in Genesis 1 made by Sjöberg is not valid. The rulers of Genesis 1 and Psalm 8 are the same—in both cases the First King and First Man—and, according to ancient modes of thinking, their descendants too. We see from Psalm 72 that in the early days of Israel the king is regarded as achieving the fertility of Paradise. Ideas of Paradise and of Primordial Man have, therefore, been connected with Israelite kingship, as it is known in the Psalms and related texts. Accordingly, it is not justifiable to regard these ideas in the "Messianic" Psalms, in Isaiah and Micah as "secondary".

The descriptions of the "First Man" found in the Old Testament (Ezekiel 28: 1–10, 11–19; Job 15: 7ff.), most certainly that in Ezekiel, point to a king. The text in Ezekiel uses mythical conceptions of the First Man in a description of the Tyrian king.[6] He lives on the "Mountain of the Gods", like the Son of God in Psalms 2 and 110.[7] The superhuman glory with which the royal First Man is here clothed, corresponds so closely to the divine *doxa* of the Son of Man of later ages, that it is not enough to say (as Mowinckel does)[8] that ideas of the

First Man and the ideas of the Messiah have no common root and that the Primordial Man is a figure which has acquired features of the common Oriental idea of the king through a combination taking place in later Judaism. This combination took place comparatively early. When the "Messiah" of the Old Testament and the conception of the king in the Psalms still seem to be "earthly" to a certain degree, the reason is that they have been influenced by the anti-Canaanite reaction referred to above. We find the same influence in the tendency to "devaluate" the divine traits in the conception of the king. For example, it is significant that the myth in Ezekiel 28[9] exhibits a consistent series of "glosses" which criticize the Oriental king ideology as it certainly existed in the Phoenician city-states.[10] It is true that Adam of Genesis 1–2, Ezekiel 28 and Job 15: 7f. is no expression of the idea of Macro- and Microcosmos (like the Scandinavian primordial giant Ymir and the Iranian Gayomard), but he has a meaning and a significant position among the ideas of the creation of the world. He is—in the terminology of Arthur Christensen[11]—*"premier homme"*, and I think we might also call him a *"prototype de l'humanité"*. Being created "after the image of God" (which according to Mowinckel[12] is used of the *"Urmensch"* and of the Mesopotamian kings), the Adam of the Old Testament may be called, in my opinion, a variant of the idea of "Primordial Man".[13] I therefore incline to the conclusion that there is a closer connection in the Old Testament between "Messiah" and "First Man" than Mowinckel assumes.

In this connection, it is not without interest that Psalm 8 calls the king "Son of Man". This is also the case in Psalm 80: 18, where the expression is used in parallel to "the man of your right hand" (cf. Psalm 110: 1).[14] That Ezekiel is also apostrophized in this way may be an expression of the fact that the royal ideology could be used also of the Patriarchs of prophetic circles.

I think, therefore, there is justification for assuming that the Israelite king of early days could be called "Messiah" without the special "eschatological" flavour now attached to the word, and that he could be described in terms of the "First Man", according to the Near Eastern variety of this figure, before any

Iranian elements began to influence Israel. The king is divine;
he is called "God" (*'ēl*) and "Son of God". We have also seen
that it is probable that The Psalms of Lamentation speak of
his sufferings, though not of his "real" death. In the combat
against the Evil Powers, he is seized by the hands of Death,
but he is saved through the mighty intervention of Yahweh. In
Psalm 132, we also find the idea that he came to the help of
Yahweh and that this led to his sufferings.

We must now stress the fact that though we have found the
king described as the "First Man" (and we may add that, in
this capacity, he is not only "*prototype de l'humanité*", but in
many other important respects "the beginning of everything"),
it is the idea of the First Man which has priority. "First Man"
in Genesis 2–3 is the "fate" of Man. The Yahwist here described
how the First Ruler of the World became its evil fate,[15] in
what is clearly an anti-Canaanite version of the idea of the
first king.

We must now ask whether it is right to think of "king
ideology" as the all-embracing category, as is generally done.
At the end of my book, *Det sakrale kongedömme*, I said that what
is called "kingship" is often more comprehensive than that
word in common speech to-day and embraces more than is
understood by "kingship" in historical times. The original
concept was earlier than the differentiation of the functions of
kings, priests, prophets, wonderworkers, healers, seers, etc. I
asked myself whether it would not be more appropriate to find
an idea expressing the fact that all such functions belong not
to a "king", but to a "primordial man" in whom the life of the
social group, the clan, the tribe, etc., is concentrated. The word
"king" suggests too narrow a range of associations and it
scarcely covers the great variety of meanings given to this
central figure in the different cultures of the world. I proposed,
therefore, the choice of another name, and I pointed out that
the Sumerian LU GAL, "the Great man", which signifies the
king,[16] might satisfy all the demands. This "First Man" is
the origin of the functions of king, prophet and priest. In the
eschatological "Man" they are again united, in what theologians later called "*munus triplex Christi*".

To this earlier treatment (retained in the German edition of the present work), I should now add the view that this meaning "First Man" must be seen in the light of the Semitic idea of the *Patriarch*.

The idea of the Patriarch has been defined in a Swedish work by H. S. Nyberg (1941).[17] The nation, the tribe, or the social group is a combination of families which are regarded as interrelated through common descent from the same ancestor. This ancestor is a mythical being—either a divinized hero or a local numen, or (most frequently) a hero identified with a local numen. The cult of the divinized ancestor is most intimately connected with the ancient Semitic cult of the dead ancestors. In Western Semitic languages, these are called *'amm*; in Arabic the word means especially "paternal uncle"; but in Hebrew it is used in its original meaning of "ancestors", as in the well-known phrase "to be gathered to his fathers" (Genesis 25: 8, Judges 2: 10, of which the first passage uses *'ammâw*, the second *'abôtâw*). Of these ancestors, the First Patriarch is the most revered and, accordingly, in its concentrated religious significance, *'amm* denotes the god of the tribe or its divinized eponymous hero. But on the other hand, because the Fathers are thought of as actually living in the existing tribe, forming an organic unity with it, the meaning of *'amm* can also be extended to denote the entire "collective" of those who are related by descent from the common Ancestor, whether living or dead. So it is that the word *'amm* comes to denote "tribe" and, in the plural, both "tribes" and "kinsmen". This is the usual meaning of the word in the Old Testament.

The primitive Semitic idea was, however, complicated in Israel. This social group is no simple clan with its clan cult. Israel was no clan, but a coalition of tribes, an "amphictyony", as M. Noth is fond of calling it. This coalition had a god, Yahweh from Sinai, who was quite different from the gods of the usual kind of ancestor worship. The connection with this god was not founded on a marriage between the first Ancestor and the divinized First Mother of the tribe, who was identical with the tribe itself. The relations between Israel and Yahweh had been inaugurated through the act of the Covenant concluded at Sinai. This factor forced the original tribal ancestor gods into the background, but the ancient idea of the marriage of the Ancestor God could not be obliterated. It was combined with the idea of the covenant to make the religious idea of the marriage-covenant between Yahweh and Israel. Yahweh could not be described as the physical father of Israel, and so he became the lover of Israel, who seeks his bride, finds her, takes care of her, protects and keeps her, and inaugurates a legitimate covenant with her. This is the background of the idea that religious defection is adultery.

The idea of Patriarchs in the old sense nevertheless lived on in the traditions concerning the origin of tribes, nations, families and professions, as we know them from Genesis. The same idea is also found behind the notion of the "Patriarch" of the Human Race, the First Man, who is, as we have seen, also the First King. In the Royal House of Jerusalem, David, of course, takes the place of a Patriarch, as he is called in Acts 2: 29. The founders of prophetic congregations were also of the same type.[18]

In Canaan, Israel took over the king ideology of the city culture of the Ancient East, and we must suppose that the Davidic dynasty adopted the usual Canaanite Adonis-conceptions, and that, for example, the penitence of the king was an established element in the annual enthronement festival.[19] During the time of the Monarchy, Israel was rent by the unresolved antagonisms between the tribal ideas of the Desert, the theocratic idea represented by the priests and prophets, and the Canaanized kingship. The monarchy probably identified itself with the tribal hero, Jacob or Israel. But at the same time, earlier ideas of the presence of famous religious heroes, looked upon as Ancestor figures, like Moses and Samuel, dominate the thoughts of the people (Psalm 99: 6, cf. Jeremiah 15: 1). Such ideas are certainly connected with ancient Canaanite thoughts of primordial kings, founders of dynasties and founders of cults, like Noah, Daniel and Job in Ezekiel 14. The Patriarchal ideology of nomadic Israel was changed through the two Canaanite influences—the ideology of the King and the ideology of the Founders of Dynasties and Cults. In this connection, Nyberg emphasizes that the term "Servant of Yahweh" is especially used of the cult-founder Moses, of the dynasty-founder David, and of Joshua, who is a parallel to Moses.

Further, he refers to KRT and Dan'el in the Ras Shamra texts, who are both described as founders of cults and dynasties, and who are styled *'abd 'Êl*. He supposes that the title "Servant of Yahweh" was an Israelite adaptation of an ancient Canaanite title, which was especially given to such persons. In earlier literature, the title is mostly used of patriarchal figures of desert type, like Abraham and Caleb. Later, it is used of Israel and Jacob; but it is also used of Isaiah (ch. 20: 3), who was the founder of a prophetic circle.

In proposing the wide designation of "First Man" or "Patriarch" as the comprehensive word to supplant the "king ideology", I have in mind especially these ideas of Nyberg. As we shall see, they will come into our picture again in the next section of this work.

We return now to the figure of the king. It is impossible to deny that these ideas are of great theological significance. The ancient Israelite "Messiah" comprises in this way several features which reappear in the New Testament and in the Church's picture of Christ—His coming forth from Eternity, Primordial Time, as the *Natus ante omnia Saecula*, His status as Son of God, the idea of Primordial Man, the *Descensus ad Inferos*, the Return from the Land of Death, the Ascension to His heavenly throne at the right hand of Yahweh, and so on. We might also mention the priestly and prophetic functions referred to in Psalms 2 and 110 and the historical descriptions of David and Solomon, which show them functioning as priests, receiving oracles of the ephod and by incubation, and invested with the gift of poetry and wisdom. The sufferings of the "Messiah" also belong to this complex. We have to notice, however, that there seems to be only a certain degree of "atoning" force in these sufferings. In this respect, we can point only to the invocation of the sufferings of David (Psalm 132: 1ff.). Here, the king is not really *dying* for his people, but fighting for it against the powers of Evil. Also in the Patriarchal idea, especially in the figure of Moses, we find the theme of intercession.

This leads us to an investigation of the "Songs of the Suffering Servant of Yahweh" in Deutero-Isaiah. How are they to be seen in relation to the "King Ideology"?

# 6

## THE SERVANT OF YAHWEH

*King or Prophet?*

THE so-called "Servant Songs" in the Deutero-Isaianic chapters of the Book of Isaiah present problems which appear less soluble than most.[1] The question of the eunuch in Acts 8: 34 was, it is true, answered by Philip, the evangelist, and by the Church. But scholars still differ very much in their opinions. It is doubtful whether they will ever arrive at the answer of the Church. For the answer of the Church will always be "an interpretation of faith", whereas, "from a strictly scientific viewpoint 'Ebed Yahweh can, of course, not be considered a direct prediction of *Jesus* Christ".[2] That Jesus of Nazareth is the "fulfilment" of these promises can only be said "in faith". It cannot be proved. We can state historically that Jesus of Nazareth must have considered Isaiah 53 the programme of His life and that He found God's plan concerning Himself in these Old Testament words. But the personal conviction that He was in fact right in hearing God's call to Himself through these words can come only by faith in Him as the Messiah and in God as His Lord. Whether we shall ever come to a clear decision in scientific terms must—in view of the never-ending discussion—remain uncertain.

The development of interpretation will not be described here, even in the most simple way.[3] The advantage about the problem as far as the history of interpretation goes is that every specialist and even beginners know the main lines of it.

In the present work, Engnell's energetic study will be taken as the starting point. The chief feature of this treatment is that he considers the "king ideology" to be the essential factor for the interpretation of the Servant Songs.[4]

This determines his understanding of the figure of the 'Ebed Yahweh and leads to a clear "Messianic" interpretation. That does not mean that he accepts a *direct* Messianic Promise in the poems,[5] which he rightly calls "an interpretation of *faith*" Further, he understands the 'Ebed Yahweh as the fulfiller of the promises to the *Davidic dynasty*. But the most distinctive feature in his picture of the Suffering Servant-type of Messianism, realized concretely in the 'Ebed Yahweh figure, lies in its strong emphasis on the aspect of suffering,[6] which is "from the very outset a legitimate and integral item of the Messianic world of thinking, belief, and cult" (i.e. of the king ideology). On the other hand, he finds no important influence from the Ancestor or "Primeval Man" ideology, although he also calls this "an inherent motif in the royal ideology".[7] He also repudiates the interpretation of the Servant figure in terms of prophetic circles or single prophetic personalities. He admits in some places a relation to Cyrus, but only as a bye-motif.[8] The essential point is that 'Ebed Yahweh is the Messiah.

Before I turn to the major problems, I find it necessary to discuss some special items of Engnell's treatment of the Songs.

First, in view of the aspect of suffering in the Psalms of Lamentation, as we discussed it in the previous chapter, I must withdraw the objection which Engnell quotes from my commentary on Isaiah 11, that "we have no evidence that the suffering of the king plays any rôle in the Israelite ritual".[9] There are psalms which can best be interpreted in that way, even if some of the examples quoted by Engnell[10] are still in my view questionable. But is it possible to use the royal ideology so exclusively in the interpretation of the Servant Songs as Engnell does?

When he concludes that the first song, *42: 1ff.*, is well fitted into the surrounding context, I am in complete agreement. I tried to prove that in my commentary and Engnell has accepted the result.[11] But it follows from my premises that the Servant of Yahweh is a prophet and is described as such in ch. 42. The word *mᵉbassêr*[12] (41: 27), which points forward to 42: 1, seems to be a term denoting an oracle-giver, a prophet. But it has also long been obvious to me[13] that there is a stylistic connection between the Servant Songs and the Royal Psalms.[14] Accordingly, I also agree with Engnell's judgment that Isaiah 42: 1 is an "ideological shaping" of the cultic reality given in

D

Psalm 2: 7.[15] Of course v. 7, the word concerning the liberation
of prisoners, may also belong to the royal ideology, as confirmed
by Accadian parallels. The expression *bᵉrît 'amm* in v. 6 may
equally be connected with royal terminology.[16] And it is right
to take the entire 42: 1–12 as one piece, not as two, as is done
by Mowinckel, following Haller. But, on the other hand, I
think that Mowinckel is right in rejecting the conclusion drawn
by Engnell from these and other "royal" features, that the
person described must necessarily be a king.[17] The parallel
adduced by Mowinckel from the description of the call of
Jeremiah proves that the stylistic forms are the same in the
oracles of calling for both kings and prophets.

If other evidence leads to the conclusion that the Servant is
a prophet, then it cannot be rejected on purely formal grounds,
nor can it be called a *petitio principii*.[18] Moreover, it is still
somewhat puzzling to me to see how the words on the blindness
and deafness of the Servant (42: 18f.) can be used as an
element of the king ideology;[19] and, at all events, the Servant
is not described in this manner in 50: 5ff. In my commentary,
following the earlier works of Mowinckel, I have assumed that
in this passage we have a description of the Servant with
the "collective" aspect in the foreground. The Servant here
carries "the pains of the people" (cf. 53: 4). But the solution of
the other problem, that a prophet is described in terms of
royal ideology, is in my opinion best solved on the assumption
that both king and prophet (as also priest) are aspects of the
comprehensive idea of a "primordial Ancestor", or
"Patriarch".[20]

In 43: 1ff., Engnell finds another "royal protection oracle".
He interprets the *'dm* of v. 4 as "Man" with the same meaning
as the Sumerian LUGAL, Accadian *amelu*.[21] The parallelism
emphatically precludes this idea. It may be right to say that
the gathering together of the dispersed is a royal-Messianic
motif, but the king is not mentioned here at all. On the contrary, the sole agent here is Yahweh and the assumed royal
motif can only be combined with him. It is different in 49: 5,
where the agent used by Yahweh is expressly mentioned. That
is not the case in 43: 1ff. for the "I" is the same in all verses.
The "Messiah" may be implicit, but he is not named. The

royal reminiscences in 44: 1ff. are more distinct and they are
of the same style as 43: 1ff. But here it is the people who is called
Servant of the Lord. At most we can say that the royal terms
are used of the people; the 'Ebed Yahweh is not a messianic
king. Engnell, however, also finds strong signs of "Tammuz
ideology" here, especially in v. 3 where the pouring out of
water and of the spirit are found in parallelism. I am not so
sure of this. Need we go further back than to Genesis 1: 2,
where we also have both water and spirit as life-giving
elements? That the creation legend again is connected with
very ancient myths of Paradise, where Adam rules as royal
gardener in primeval days, is quite possible;[22] but then this
only shows us that the ancient elements are so old that we have
seriously to question whether they retained their original
meaning for the man who composed the Deutero-Isaianic
"liturgy".

Whether the name *Jeshurun* in v. 2 is clearly related precisely to the "Tammuz ideology",[23] I leave undecided. It
is also possible that the parallelism in v. 5 could be understood
as using the two names Jacob and Israel as synonyms for
Yahweh, i.e. as divine names (cf. Psalm 24: 6). But again, I
doubt whether Deutero-Isaiah was conscious of this meaning.
Engnell's temptation to assume an error of the ear in v. 4 and
so interpret as "and one rejoices over 'the Son of Verdure' ", I
personally find no difficulty in resisting. It looks like an out-
burst of the *"rabies emendationum"* which Engnell so often—and
so rightly—attacks.[24] To suppose that a Jewish prophet of the
sixth century consciously spoke in such a positive manner of
Tammuz is simply monstrous (cf. Ezekiel 8: 14).

I agree with Engnell[25] in his rejection of the assumption of a
gloss in 45: 4*a*, but the severely national limitation of Deutero-
Isaiah[26] is not, however, proved. There is a universalism in
Deutero-Isaiah which is taken over from the Enthronement
Psalms, where the world dominion of Yahweh and his Anointed
is proclaimed. The other traces of king ideology in the Cyrus
oracles are of course rightly noted by Engnell. But this is well
known and of no relevance for the interpretation of the Servant
as a royal Messiah. The Cyrus oracle of 45: 1ff. is, of course,
worded in the style of the royal psalms.[27] Again, however, I

think it necessary to issue a warning against being too certain about the direct Babylonian background of Deutero-Isaiah. If Engnell intends to say that 46: 1ff. reflects what the prophet saw in the streets of Babylon and no more, then I can agree completely. But if he means that the prophet took a "positive" interest in Babylonian cults, then I must disagree. But it seems that his aim is only to stress the fact that Deutero-Isaiah lived in Babylon.[28]

In *49: 1–13*, the second Servant Song, we must distinguish several oracles, but taken as a whole they describe the task of the Servant. So far I agree with Engnell. Here, the Servant is clearly described as leader of the New Exodus from Babylon.[29]

This important "prophetic confession" or "autobiographical story"[30] is treated very summarily by Engnell. He is limited, by the plan of his work, to noting the phrases which must be regarded as being marked by king ideology. But we have already seen that such phrases in similar contexts (cf. ch. 42: 1ff. and Jeremiah) are used of prophets. I agree with Engnell[31] that the word "Israel" in v. 3 is not necessarily a "gloss" on metrical and text-critical grounds,[32] but I cannot agree when he rejects my arguments[33] simply by means of his slogan "logicism". It is just on the basis of the "inner logicality" of the assumption that the Servant identifies himself with his people that it is possible to retain the word. That would be "logicism" too. My rejection of the word is due to my impression that, on the whole, it is badly supported in our texts, as also in 42: 1.[34] I admit that it may be possible to regard the word as "genuine", even if the poem describes the Servant as chosen for a special task in the history of Israel (vv. 5–6). He may be called Israel as the incarnation of the first Ancestor of the people, and as such he may be the bearer of Yahweh's salvation to his "children",[35] just as the Davidic king may have been identified with the ancestors of the nation.[36] From this presupposition, it would be "logical" to deduce the "genuineness" of the disputed word. But in general it is uncertain in our texts and so I doubt its originality.

What Engnell does not touch upon in this connection is what interests me personally, namely the view that the Servant is here described as "a new Moses".[37] How this fits in with king ideology we shall see later. That the word "Servant" is used of the king, I do not deny in view of the many important quotations he gives (*op. cit.* p. 18, n. 41). Of course, Engnell knows that it is also used of people other than the king. But I explain the cases otherwise.[38]

Engnell mainly follows my ideas about the composition of *50: 4–11*.[39] It is a Psalm of Lamentation with a strongly-emphasized consciousness of innocence. Engnell tries to prove that it is a Royal Psalm, but with more stress on the "Tammuz-motives" than the earlier poems. The contention that "already *ᵃdônâj* in v. 5 gives an intimation of the royal categories" I cannot accept as satisfactory, even though there may be some justification for the view.[40] It is too general a word in the Old Testament to be used in this manner here, unless other important evidence supports the suggestion. In the following words, Engnell wishes to give the term *limmûdîm* "a special meaning", connected with divination. He refers to a very obscure text, 2 Samuel 1: 18, which he is tempted to combine with Isaiah 49: 2, taking the root to mean "to sting".[41] I cannot see how it is methodologically justifiable to build far-reaching conclusions on a text like 2 Samuel 1: 18; nevertheless, the word may have some connection with divination, and this would lead us into a prophetic track. Here, as before, the king ideology is not the sole possibility, even if the thesis be accepted that "the king was in principle the only oracle receiver, the divination often taking place in the morning after a foregoing night of incubation".[42] Again, the matter is uncertain. The expression "in principle" suggests uncertainty, and in the Old Testament it is not true even "in principle", but only in some few cases. Prophetic circles and their spiritual exercises (1 Samuel 19: 18ff.) illustrate our text just as well.

The same is the case with v. 6. Of course, I am aware of its association with the scene in the Babylonian New Year festival, where the king is humiliated by the priest. But I also remember my associations with the pædagogic methods of the ancient schools and I cannot rule them out as easily as Engnell does. In the following chapter, the interpretation of 51: 18 on the basis of Amenemope (ed. Lange, Copenhagen, 1925, pp. 125f.) is more appropriate, and so also it is here,[43] or, at least, it suggests a possibility just as good as the royal ideology. In both cases, the meaning is the same. The Servant of Yahweh in the school of his master has obtained teaching against which he has not rebelled (vv. 4–5)—namely that his path will lead to suffering (v. 6). The ultimate connection of this with a Tammuz ideology is of antiquarian interest, but not much more. The following "lawsuit motif" is also combined with the king ideology and so the problem of the psalms called by Hans Schmidt *Gebete der Angeklagten*, prayers of accused persons, is brought before us.

I do not think that Hans Schmidt's idea can be rejected *a limine*. It has to be treated, in some cases at least (Psalm 107: 10–16), as a reasonable possibility.[44] The "typical royal third person style" in 10–11*b* and "the royal suffering ideology in its special infernal aspect" in v. 10*b* may have been originally connected with the royal ritual, like the corresponding descriptions in the Psalms of Lamentation of the king and the suffering innocents. But, in Deutero-Isaiah's day, the "democratization of the ritual" must have been so developed that this question cannot be answered unequivocally. Here, the context must decide whether the Servant of the Lord should be regarded as king or as prophet, and the example of Jeremiah's inaugural vision must be decisive.

Concerning *52: 13 – 53: 12*, I must again express my agreement in principle with Engnell's treatment of the problem of the tenses in this text: the whole poem speaks of the future.[45] The description of the fate of the Servant must be viewed from the "ideal" standpoint of the contemporary witnesses of his life and death.[46] But I cannot go so far as to say that it is not an historical person whose fate is described. I take the view it *is* an historical person, whose future fate is described. I might even say that the Servant here prophesies his own fate and expresses his hope. It is a parallel to the Gospel predictions of the death and resurrection of Jesus.[47] The death and rehabilitation of the Servant are prophetically described from the point of view of witnesses, who discovered that they had been completely mistaken in their judgment of this prophet. I cannot deny the possibility that a contemporary of the prophet or the prophet himself could be regarded as a sort of "Messiah", or that the prophet could think of himself in this way.[48] Concerning form-critical questions also I agree with Engnell:[49] the poem has the form of a *liturgy*, consisting of many elements from different types of poetry. Engnell is quite right in stressing that "owing to its peculiarity as regards both motif and situation, it cannot be ranked with any of Gunkel's usual categories". There is a mixture of categories in it, as is also stressed by Mowinckel.[50]

Our agreement is broken only in connection with less important matters. Engnell's thoughts concerning the *jaskîl* of 52: 13 are interesting. He understands it as denoting "the act of taking possession of the throne". The interpretation seems well-founded, although not all the passages quoted as proof are quite valid. Especially significant is the passage Daniel 12: 3, where the royal position of the beatified "Wise" is characterized by this expression, and it also has parallels in the New Testament. The compilation of parallels from the Tammuz songs, which Engnell makes for the illustration of v. 14, is very important. They really prove that these traditional features mean something for the description of the Servant. Only we must again ask, was this really understood by the Jewish prophet of the sixth century? This is what Engnell seems to mean, at least in the Swedish form of his article. In the English version, he has added[51] some more material from the Ugaritic texts, and some very pointed and well-balanced remarks, which I wish to quote: "We must add, however, that the whole perspective has become completely changed. We see now that it is not a question of a superficial influence from outside, from Babylonia, but of an idea autochthonic with the Western Semites, too, inherently bound up with the sacral kingship pattern in Canaan, and taken over there by Israel. Thus, the adducing of Sumero-Accadian parallels here must not be misunderstood, and by no means put on a level with the working method of the so-called pan-Babylonists (a fatality remarkably enough easily met with by a 'patternist'; . . .). The parallels are not even intended to show a direct Accadian influence; they 'merely' support, as pointed out once before, a factual internally Israelite world of thoughts with a distinctive cultic background".[52] But the antiquarian material makes

little contribution to the question debated here—Is the Servant
king or prophet?—since the expressions are used of both. In
wider religio-historical and theological connections, these
mythological features have, on the other hand, great
significance.

In his treatment of 52: 15, Engnell has some very good
remarks concerning the old *crux interpretum, yazzeh*,[53] which he
explains for once on the basis of the LXX translation, and
from the well-known Arabic root *naza* and the formal parallel
49: 7.

On 53: 1, Engnell criticizes me for disputing Nyberg's interpretation of the word *šemûʻâh* with the remark that an "ancient
myth" could not have surprised the onlookers to the degree
indicated here. I am fully aware that "the mysterious message
of the ancient cult myth is, contemporaneously, always new,
i.e. experienced over and over again".[54] Engnell is right in
supposing that my criticism was to some extent caused by
"Nyberg's too mythologizing interpretation". Although I cannot fully agree with Engnell, I am very much obliged to him
for his strictures and for the stimulus he has given me to think
over the passage again. Nyberg thinks that the word *šemûʻâh*,
*auditum*, here means "What was heard by us", i.e. "the tradition which we have received". The following part of the poem
accordingly is regarded as the sacred tradition concerning the
person described in it, the Servant of Yahweh. My argument
against Nyberg was that the story told in the following verses,
the passion and resurrection story of the Servant of the Lord,
is regarded in the preceding verses of the liturgy as something
*absolutely new*—as the Germans say, *"etwas noch nie Dagewesenes"*.
The translation "tradition" is misleading, because it does not
do justice to this important *nuance* in the poem. In this connection, it makes no difference that "the mysterious message of
the ancient cult myth is, contemporaneously, always new, i.e.
experienced over and over again". I know that very well, both
from a study of the history of religions and from practical
life. The idea of Gyllenberg, that Deutero-Isaiah's book is an
imitation of a liturgy for the New Year Festival, is very possibly right,[55] and that Isaiah 53, in this connection, describes
the passion and resurrection of the "Messiah". This was the idea

of the "ancient myth" which has been replaced, in the imitation of the liturgy, by the fourth 'Ebed Yahweh Song of Deutero-Isaiah.

But in the process by which the "ancient myth" has been replaced by the poem in Isaiah 53, something has happened that is not expressed in the translation "tradition". The poet wants to say that the story of the rehabilitation of the Servant of the Lord is something new, not only a "remembrance", *anamnesis*, of the old well-known gospel, but a new event of epoch-making importance. The ideas of "newness" which underlie the poem are not "new" as they are interpreted in the New Year Festival psalms, when they speak of a "new song" (Psalms 96: 1; 98: 1; 149: 1), indicating that the cycle of the year has begun again and that the world is again secure through the enactment of the rites. What is told in Isaiah 53 is the *absolutely New*, in the sense which this word has got in its setting, that is, throughout the prophet's preaching. Deutero-Isaiah here makes use of old forms taken over from the New Year Festival and also ideas of the "re-creation" of the world. But he does so in a way quite different from that of the old cult hymns, the pattern of which he uses as a model for his own. In his poems he not only speaks of the re-iteration in the cult of the "old" reality of creation, or—what to Israel is the same—the Exodus from Egypt. The "New" here is something far greater than that which was experienced in the "old" festival "over and over again".

The conception of Deutero-Isaiah must be compared with the ideas in the (probably anonymous) passage in the book of Jeremiah (31: 31ff.), which speaks of the "New Covenant" destined to replace the "Old Covenant" from the days of Moses. We miss this point if, with Nyberg, Engnell and Mowinckel, we only use the word "tradition" and talk about the sources of the poems in ancient Oriental cult myths.

To understand the meaning of Deutero-Isaiah, it is of major importance to perceive clearly his idea of the contrast, or perhaps better, the parallelism, between the "Old" and the "New". Here, it is also necessary to perceive the full weight of the '*al-tizkerû*, "remember not the former things, neither consider the things of old", of 43: 18. The word *zkr*—as we all know[56]—denotes not only our usual sense of "remembrance", but also creative "remembrance" in the cult, which causes the Holy Past to live again, bringing its vital forces into the congregation. That is what we must find if we use the translation, "tradition", of *šemû'âh*. But Deutero-Isaiah exhorts his people not to look back any longer to the Holy Past of the Exodus from Egypt. For they now experience new events which are to be the creative contents of a new cult myth, the new Exodus from Babylonia.[57] This thought finds expression in the passion story in ch. 53 and also in the single Hebrew word discussed here. Therefore, I think that my objection to the translation of Nyberg is even more correct than I perceived myself, when I wrote those words in my commentary which are criticized by Engnell.

This Deutero-Isaianic idea of the "New" has parallels in New Testament eschatology; we need only remember 2 Corinthians 5: 17*b* and Revelation 21: 5. Deutero-Isaiah presupposes here something similar to the Jewish and the New Testament idea of "this world" and "the world to come". He expresses a definitely "eschatological" view of history. This eschatological element seems to be neglected by both my Swedish colleagues.[58] The translation "tradition" in Isaiah 53: 1 is misleading then, in so far as it does not do justice to the eschatological element in the Deutero-Isaianic imitation of the New Year liturgy.

It is easier to criticize the translation of others than to supply another. Instead of "the tradition which we have received", it would be better, in my opinion, to return to the version rejected by Nyberg, "the *revelation* which we have received". To this extent I agree with Nyberg; we should not think primarily that the term denotes something "heard" by the prophet, an audition; even though, of course, an experience of prophetic-poetical inspiration does underlie Deutero-Isaiah's poems. We should perhaps render the words better by translating "the *gospel* which we have received", or "which has just now been revealed to us".

In my paper on the Story of the Ark[59] in the *Journal of Biblical Literature* (1948), I drew attention to the remarkable phenomenon that, in the age of David, especially after his liberation of Israel from the yoke of the Philistines, there seems to have been an inclination to form a new cult myth. I interpreted the story of the Ark as connected with the cult myth—based on historical experiences—of the festival inaugurated by David in Jerusalem and later imitated by Jeroboam I in order to compete with the Jerusalem festival. This is an expression of the "historifying" tendency in Israelite religion, first seen in the Exodus story, which is an "historification" of the myth of creation. It is certain that this tendency also lies behind the story of the patriarchs, which we have as a parallel to the traditions of Moses. The great events of history always had a tendency to become "myths" in the religious perception of Israel. By "myths" here I mean "gospels", expressions of the revelation of the creative, vital forces of God. I think that we must understand, for example, the stories of the defeat of Sennacherib before Jerusalem as expressions of the same tendency. This is the truth in the idea of earlier criticism that the Psalms of the Enthronement are to be combined historically with this event. These psalms, however, give us not the results, but the ideological presuppositions of the stories.

This tendency to "historification" was also active in the age of the decline and fall of the Israelite and Judaean kingdoms. It reveals itself in the Sennacherib stories and it also comes to light in the expectation of a "New Covenant", as expressed in Jeremiah 31: 31. It is against this background also that we must understand Deutero-Isaiah and his expectations of events which will create a "New Myth", destined to replace the "Ancient Myth" of the Exodus festival. He also expects a "New Covenant".

This notion of the "New Covenant" received its epoch-making interpretation when it was used by Jesus to transform the Passover meal of Judaism into an expression of the "New Myth" created by the historical events of His own death and resurrection. Here He took up the idea of the Servant of the Lord in Deutero-Isaiah. If this chapter is regarded as the "gospel" of the congregation assembled round the prophet Deutero-Isaiah—and I think it is so[60]—then the expectations of that circle of disciples have received their fulfilment in the "gospel" of the Church.[61]

Concerning 53: 1ff., Engnell is inclined to think that the

Servant's own countrymen first and foremost constitute the speakers, but that the "many peoples" are also included among them. On this point I will not enter into controversy. In 53: 2, he finds himself in a Tammuz passage which is clearer than ever. The scion is the tree or plant of life, a symbol of the king Tammuz—in this context, during the time of withering, i.e. in the aspect of suffering. I am not quite sure of this.[62] I think that Mowinckel is right when he says that imagery of the withering tree cannot everywhere be counted as evidence for a connection with Tammuz ideas.[63] The Wisdom literature uses the image in more general applications, as we know from the material which is adduced to illustrate Psalm 1. It may of course be assumed that the Wisdom literature got the imagery from the Tammuz ideology, but that would only lead us to the ideas of "democratization" and "disintegration" and to the factual contents of Mowinckel's criticism. I conclude, therefore, that here also Engnell's words are too emphatic.

On the other hand, I again agree with him when he rejects the theory that the Servant was a leper. Under the influence of Nyberg's article,[64] I myself went too far in this direction. Guillaume's arguments against this idea,[65] that lepers were untouchable, and that the theory therefore is incompatible with the descriptions of the scourging and plucking out of his beard in 50: 4ff. and 53, are decisive. It is also true that *nega‘* does not always mean leprosy. On the other hand, I cannot allow that the argument from the Tammuz texts which do not exhibit this feature carries the decisive weight given to it by Engnell. This is an invalid *argumentum e silentio*.

The idea of *vicarious suffering* dominates the rest of the poem. This is again taken as an expression of the influence of the royal ritual and as proof of Engnell's thesis that the Servant is the king Messiah. That this is only partly the right interpretation we shall see later. The same is the case with the metaphor of the Servant as a shepherd, presupposed in 53: 6, which is said to be "the ancient epithet of the sacral king as well as of Tammuz". The figure of the lamb is, of course, connected with the Mari and Ras Shamra texts and their ideas of this animal as a substitution for any sacrifice for the Tammuz-king, of which the most important Old Testament form is met with in the ritual of the Day of Atonement.[66] This again is thought to depend upon the royal ritual, as also the *motif* of the "cultic silence" found in v. 7: the king or his representative must at some parts of the ritual observe a dignified silence, in others cry aloud. This *motif* is also found in Jeremiah 11: 19, in a description of the prophet.

I think we must conclude from this that, as far as the interpretation of our text goes, Engnell's explanation, in concluding that we have a royal ritual scene,[67] rests on too narrow a basis. The same is true of his remarks on v. 8. He takes the words *mê' ôser ûmimmišpāt* to be a *hendiadys*, translating "a judgment of violence". He begins by stating that the meaning is not quite certain and that he has in reserve a meaning quite different from the theories of Nyberg and Guillaume which he cannot enlarge upon. But after all these moments of uncertainty, he concludes quite unreservedly that the meaning of this *hendiadys* is to point to the passion of the sacral king. The king is conceived as standing in a lawsuit in which he is condemned, although innocent, for the sins of the people. Here I refer again to the comments on the Prayers of the Accused given above and stress that there are other possible explanations.

Equally uncertain is the association of the verb *nigzar* in v. 8 with the Tammuz ideology and the idea of the king as the tree of life. The same may be said of the description of the funeral in v. 9. I think that Engnell's rejection of historical features from the life of the Servant, even such features as had not yet been fulfilled, but were threatening prospects, is the main defect here. In v. 9 he is again tempted to make an emendation and to read *bâmâtô* for *bᵉmôtâw*.[68] In v. 10b he follows Nyberg;[69] *heḥᵉlî* is not understood as sickness, but taken from a root *ḥlh*, in the hiphil, as a transitive to the intransitive pi'el, in the sense of "to be appeased".

The following section, according to Nyberg, is difficult, because the two conceptions of "pledge" and "guilt-offering" have been confused.[70] He translates: "When his soul gives a pledge consisting in a guilt-offering". Engnell, of course, refers the words of offering and libation to the Tammuz sphere. The sacrifice is the atonement sacrifice of the king who offers himself or his substitute.

In v. 10*b*, Engnell finds an abrupt switching over from the negative to the positive, from death to resurrection. He rightly rejects Nyberg's opinion that "seed" is the subject of the clause. The subject must be the Servant. According to Engnell, the *motif* is to be found again and again in benedictions in Accadian royal texts. It refers to the double aspect of the victory of life over death: the individual aspect with its "eternal" life, and the collective aspect through the countless progeny to come. Parallels are found in the *Alijan Ba'al* and *Aqhat gzr* texts from Ugarit. These heroes create progeny in connection with their descent and resurrection and perhaps the same idea is found also in the KRT texts. Engnell, therefore, thinks it too narrow to see in v. 10 only a reference to the Servant's own bodily resurrection. In this connection, he criticizes the usual conception of resurrection in the Old Testament as being too much dominated by the Persian mode of thinking. This has been the cause of the late (and according to Engnell false) dating of the idea. He finds the origins in "autochthonous cult usages, bound up with the dying and rising god, and with analogies from vegetable life".[71] The words "by the knowledge of himself he maketh the righteous righteous" must be re-interpreted in some such way as: "by means of the cultic-mystic unity with the Saviour every participant shares in the realized salvation". Further, according to Engnell, this is repeated and confirmed in the conclusion of the liturgy, where Yahweh speaks again, as at the beginning. Finally, the passage 54: 1ff. is held to form a hymnic conclusion to the Servant Song—a view with which I agree.

I am less convinced by his interesting statements about the resurrection in this chapter. The recent article by Birkeland seems to me to take some of the force out of Engnell's observations. I am more inclined to follow Mowinckel's interpretation,[72] which, as far as I can see, is not very different from that of Engnell. That there is some connection between the Oriental myths and the resurrection idea seems clear. Mowinckel and Birkeland stress the differences between Israel and the surrounding religions, but both Engnell and Mowinckel end in a theory of a cultic-mystic experience in the circle gathered round the Servant of Yahweh.

The main result of this rapid survey of Engnell's interesting study is that I cannot see that the thesis of the royal status of the Servant has been definitely proved. There are many points which may be connected with king ideology,[73] but in many cases these points can also be explained in other ways. The same must be said of the Tammuz ideology; but *some* connection there seems to be. It is not, however, as strong as is thought by Engnell. Many phrases are clearly ancient clichés used traditionally by the prophet, but it is doubtful whether they retain their original meanings. Our task is to interpret them in their present, Israelite context—a task to which Engnell has also made an important contribution.

In stating my own conception, I wish first to emphasize that I consider it wrong to reject the existence of an historical person behind the figure of the 'Ebed Yahweh. In the last addition to the English edition of his article, Engnell stresses that his Messiah as the *Davidic* Messiah has a basis in real life. But I think this is not enough. We must point to an historical figure among the prophet's contemporaries. To deny the historicity of the 'Ebed Yahweh would be equal to a denial of (say) Cyrus in chapters 44–45. The 'Ebed Yahweh, in Deutero-Isaiah's thoughts, seems to be just as real and historical as the Persian king. When we accept Gyllenberg's thesis that the Deutero-Isaianic cycle of poems is an imitation of a New Year liturgy, we must bear in mind that the imitation involves some historic actualization of the myth.[74] The prophet, in composing his liturgical cycle, aimed at describing an act of Salvation taking place in his own day. Perhaps it is necessary to have experienced a liberation from enemy oppression to understand fully what that means. The *mᵉbassêr* of 41: 27 must, therefore, be just as actual and historical as Cyrus and the Babylonians, and, let us add, "David" of 55: 3ff. The situation of Deutero-Isaiah and the liberation from the Philistines in the time of David are historically analogous; and as the Story of the Ark and Psalm 132 give evidence of a "new myth", so does the Deutero-Isaianic "liturgy".

Accordingly, when we interpret the Deutero-Isaianic Servant of the Lord as the Messianic *king*, he must be identified with the heir of David alluded to in chapter 55. He must be imagined as Son of David in a concrete person, as the Jews in 520–16 identified Zerubbabel with the Messiah.[75]

These factors already give the "I" of the Servant Songs a meaning other than the purely "ideal" meaning of the king ideology, as this is applied to the Servant. According to the general rule of prophetic speech, the "I" must be either Yahweh or the prophet. The first alternative is impossible; the second is the only one which can be accepted. When we seek to understand the texts as "Messianic" in connection with the history of Deutero-Isaiah's times, we must of necessity come near to an "autobiographical" interpretation.[76] The view that the Servant could be combined with the Davidic king of 55: 3ff. seems to be out of the question, on other grounds.

We have often said that the royal ideology is not the only possible way of explaining many elements in the picture of the Servant. More especially, we have emphasized that many features are common to the texts of inauguration for both kings and prophets. Faced with this situation, Engnell has a ready answer—the king is the "primordial prophet"[77] and originally stands as the sole receiver of oracles. Against this argument we urged[78] that it is perhaps not quite satisfactory from a phenomenological standpoint to concentrate everything so narrowly around the king. The "primordial phenomenon" must be defined more broadly. For the comprehensive category we suggested the "First Man" or the "First Ancestor", the Patriarch of the Human Race. We imagine that this idea was differentiated in the various circles or social structures, as "chief", "king", "priest", "prophet", and so on. *Sheikhs* of these various kinds are very frequently invested with the same attributes, but named differently. Therefore it appears mistaken always to conclude from such attributes that the figure is a "king". It is equally justifiable to infer from such attributes that the figure is a prophet, ancestor, cult-founder, etc., as Nyberg does.

Among the expressions which Engnell especially claims as an argument for the royal Messianic character of the Servant of Yahweh is the title, '*Ebed Yahweh*.[79] Here again, it is impossible to maintain that its royal meaning is in every case established simply by the fact that it occurs in a text.[80] Nyberg, with greater judgment, has classified the aspects of the title which can be used in our work.[81] Further, he has stressed the fact that the Servant of the Lord in Deutero-Isaiah exhibits especially the features of the Ancestor—the Patriarch. He is both individual and collective. He is "Israel" in the sense both of the ancestor and of his people. In him, the life and history of a people is concentrated. But the figure here is more complicated than ever before. We are far removed from the simple art of story-telling and the naïve joy of Genesis in its description of the fates of the ancestors. New thoughts have taken over the old *motifs* and new experiences have given them new content.

These general considerations we can accept. I am also able to acknowledge that royal and Tammuz motifs have played a part in the stylistic composition of the texts, but as distant influences and through the mediation of Israelite cultic psalms, as shown by the example of Jeremiah's inaugural vision and his monologues. The most interesting feature in the observations of Nyberg is his reference to Moses, Joshua and David. These persons, he says, are more than "kings". David, like Moses, is a cult founder, above all in Chronicles, but also in earlier traditions. His relation to the foundation of the temple in Jerusalem is also quite obvious in the Books of Samuel, especially in the stories of the Ark, where he is even the founder of a myth.[82]

It is also obvious that *Moses* in Deutero-Isaiah plays an eminent rôle, a fact which is completely ignored by Engnell. Sellin, in several publications,[83] has underlined the importance of the Mosaic traditions for the Songs of the Servant of the Lord. That his idea has had no great success is, of course, due to the fantastic manner in which he drew conclusions from the Servant Songs for the history of Moses and his death at the hands of his own people—which has had a tragi-comical sequel in the work of Sigmund Freud on Moses. Sellin's novel on Moses and his death as a martyr in Transjordania has no basis in reality. These features in the picture of the Servant of the Lord are satisfactorily explained by the figure of the suffering innocent man, perhaps originally the king, in certain psalms.[84]

But, setting aside the fantastic elements, Sellin's idea of the

E

influence of the traditional picture of Moses on the Servant
Songs is worthy of consideration. The Servant is sometimes
compared with Moses or Joshua, especially in the so-called
second song (49: 5–6 and 8–12).[85] The fact that 49: 9 speaks
of the liberation of prisoners in terms of the return of Israel
shows that the assumed royal ideology is here actualized in
the circumstances of the exile. The Servant of the Lord is
described as a new Moses or Joshua, leader of the new Exodus
and of a new allotment of the land to the tribes. It must, therefore, be considered very probable that the 'Ebed Yahweh in
the scheme of Deutero-Isaiah played the rôle of the "new
Moses"—"Moses redivivus", by which I do *not* mean a reincarnate or returned Moses.[86] It is also probable that the
traditions of Moses have influenced other passages, and especially the record of the vicarious suffering of the Servant. I do
not follow Sellin in thinking that I can prove that Moses himself suffered the death of a martyr at the hands of Israel. Of
this the traditions know nothing. We cannot leave the firm
ground of the traditions of Moses and try to reconstruct the
life and death story of Moses on the basis of Isaiah 53, but
both deuteronomistic and pre-deuteronomistic traditions
describe Moses as willing to die instead of Israel (Exodus 32:
31ff.), and he is represented as the great intercessor who risks
his life to save the sinful people (Deuteronomy 9). With these
passages we may also consider Deuteronomy 1: 37; 3: 26; and
4: 21, where Moses is included in the punishment of the
people. Here we have the idea of an "inclusive" vicarious
suffering.[87]

These prefigurations of the thought of the vicarious suffering
of the Servant of Yahweh are in my opinion clearer than those
related to extra-Israelite king ideology, although undoubtedly
the idea of vicarious suffering is known also outside Israel.[88]
In the Old Testament, Engnell and Widengren find this idea
especially in the ritual of Leviticus 16.[89] In Deutero-Isaiah,
Moses as the prefiguration of vicarious suffering is described
with expressions taken from the king ideology—such would be
our compromise formula. It would, however, be more adequate
to substitute "First Man ideology" or "Patriarchal ideology"
for "king ideology", since without these wider conceptions we

cannot fully grasp the idea of 'Ebed Yahweh, in which the prophetic features are more prominent than the royal ideology.

The Servant of the Lord is a figure in whom many features are united. To regard him as future Messiah in the framework of the king ideology is too simple. On the contrary, the royal ideology—as far as it represents sacral kingship or divine kingship—is rather weakly attested in the figure of the Servant. The anti-Canaanite reaction has "demythologized" the figure of the king, and it has undergone a very radical change in Deutero-Isaiah. The Servant is no god like the ancient Israelite king. We have here one of the most radical, and later one of the most influential *Gestaltwandlungen des Erlösers* (mutations) in the history of the "Messianic" idea. The other is the figure of the "Son of Man" of later Judaism.

Finally, we must observe that with this explanation of the Deutero-Isaianic Messiah as "Moses redivivus", as the "new" Saviour in the "new" world with its "new" cult-myth, we have implicitly defined our position on the question of his relation to "David" in 55: 3ff. The "I" of the Servant Songs shows that the prophet himself takes up the task of the new Moses. That is his Call. The future "David" accordingly must be thought of as a person alongside him as leader of the restoration of Israel. Probably "David" was as historical in this period as Cyrus or the 'Ebed Yahweh. The prophet probably had in mind the great event of this period, the last event told in the Book of Kings, the liberation and rehabilitation of Jehoiachin. He thought of him or his eldest son in a way which corresponds to the expectations attached to Zerubbabel twenty-five years later. When we remember how the Exodus traditions are prototypes for Deutero-Isaiah, it seems probable that he thought of *two* leaders of the new Exodus, corresponding to Moses and Aaron, or perhaps Moses and Joshua. In this way, I think we can fill out the sketch given in my *Introduction*: The 'Ebed Yahweh is Deutero-Isaiah and Israel, the new Moses ("Messias" in radically changed form) and the congregation for whom he is ready to die, in one single person, the Patriarch of the new race.

# 7

## THE POSITION OF THE SERVANT OF YAHWEH IN THE HISTORY OF THE ISRAELITE MESSIANIC HOPE

In spite of the criticism which has been levelled against several elements of Engnell's interpretation of the 'Ebed Yahweh Songs, we must emphasize that in general we agree with him. There *is* a connection between the Songs and ancient Oriental ideology, whether we call it "king ideology" or stress to a greater degree the prophetic character of the person described in them. We have said that we prefer to use the idea of the "First Man" as the ideological central figure; perhaps it were better still to say "Patriarch". In addition, we have emphasized the "historical" character of the "Messiah" and pointed out that he was described in the picture of the vicarious suffering of Moses. To this we may add that in the main stream of Israelite tradition Moses is regarded as a prophet.[1]

This has recently been maintained by Nyberg.[1] He also rightly discovers individual features in the picture of the 'Ebed Yahweh which have, so to speak, been drawn from a living model. Such features cannot have been taken over from king ideology nor can they have been combined with an individual royal figure. Nyberg further points out that in the time and the circles in which our texts originated, kingship must have been regarded as fallen, dead and doomed. Kingship was the example *par excellence* of disobedience and defection from Yahweh. The prophetic circles would quite naturally have thought of a prophet, when they tried to imagine a person who would renew Israel. The prophets appear as founders of cults and they must have regarded themselves as such and have been acknowledged as such by others. According to Nyberg, their attitude to the cult can be understood only in this way. So they were put in the position which of old had been given to the cult founder and to the leaders of religious fraternities, the position of "religious Ancestor" or "Father". Therefore, they could be called 'Ebed Yahweh, as was Isaiah (20: 3). Further, they could compete with the king and claim to represent the Ancestor "Israel" and the people descending from him.

After the fall of kingship, nobody could dispute this claim of theirs. The temple, which had been so intimately connected with kingship, had been destroyed, and with it the claims of the priests to represent Israel. The prophets alone were left on the stage and they had to suffer all the vicissitudes of the times. The spiritual history of Israel during the exile became the history of the prophets and the prophetic circles. The second temple, however, created a new situation. Its priesthood absorbed the prophetic circles and took over their claims.

So far the ideas of Nyberg on this matter. Perhaps he under-estimates the activities of both priests and wisdom teachers during the exile, but, in the main, his account is a true one.

In my opinion, there is only one feature to be added to this picture and that is the significance of Moses as model for the 'Ebed Yahweh. Instead, Nyberg places in the foreground the tragic fate of Jeremiah, drawing attention to Jeremiah 10: 19, 21. But he also thinks of Isaiah himself, who is expressly called 'Ebed Yahweh. The book of Isaiah was, of course, says Nyberg, the canonical document of the congregation which considered Isaiah their founder and religious ancestor, or Patriarch. In this connection, Nyberg recalls the later traditions concerning the martyr death of Isaiah under Manasseh, which may very well contain an historical nucleus. Nyberg also reminds us that Euler[2] has shown that the question of the Ethiopian eunuch (Acts 8: 34) alludes to a tradition that the 'Ebed Yahweh was Isaiah himself, and that later tradition about Isaiah may well be connected with the interpretation of the text found in the LXX. Nyberg, however, thinks it irrelevant to seek for the original prophetic 'Ebed Yahweh. Perhaps the original model was not one man, but several: "an historical column which has been drawn up so straight that the single individuals cannot be distinguished from one another appears, when seen by one standing before it, as one individuality". We may have a succession of leaders of prophetic circles, among whom one

had been especially ill-treated in the catastrophic period and
had borne all his suffering with such surrender to the will of
God, that everybody was forced to recognize the liberating
and healing force of his act.

As far as I can see, Nyberg has described here something
essential in the Songs of the Servant, which is not brought out
by Engnell. We too have emphasized the element of historical
realism by saying that "the 'Ebed Yahweh is just as 'real' as
Cyrus". On reflection, we may perhaps judge that Nyberg has
eliminated the rôle of kingship too completely. Even the book of
Ezekiel counts upon a Davidic prince, and the words of Isaiah
55: 3 must certainly be understood to mean that kingship also
is to have a place in the New Israel founded by the new Moses.

But the "Messianic" figure *par excellence*, the 'Ebed Yahweh,
is in the main described not as king, but as "Moses". And
Moses is not the king, although as cult founder he is depicted
with the features of the "First Man" and "First King" ideology.
As Pedersen wrote: "Moses occupies a special position. He
who 'carries the people like a nurse' (Numbers 11: 12) has
in his position features of the king, as he was during the pros-
perous days of the monarchy of Jerusalem. *But he cannot simply
be regarded as the archetype of the king*, as Aaron is of the high
priest. Partly his figure has doubtless, as the leader of the
wilderness period, a form and character independent of the
monarchy, and it must partly have been affected by the dis-
appearance of the monarchy and the lack, in later Israel, of any
living head of the nation in whose light Moses could be viewed.
*He was something apart, a leader of primeval ages*, who spoke
directly with Yahweh (Numbers 12: 8)."[3] As Moses in the
"Old Myth" was the cult founder and leader of the Exodus,
so the 'Ebed Yahweh occupies the same position in the "New
Myth". He is the "New Moses". And this leader of the Israel
of the new world age is the Prophet of the Return, Deutero-
Isaiah himself.

The most peculiar feature of the 'Ebed Yahweh figure over
against the more ancient king ideology in Israel is the remarkable *absence of all divine attributes*. Many expressions are used
which point back to Royal Psalms. But the Servant of the
Lord is never called "God", like the king in Psalm 45, or the

Messianic king in Isaiah 9: 5. In such passages we still perceive the divine *doxa* of the ancient Oriental King, just as in the formulary of Isaiah 7: 14 and 11: 1ff. Divine features are also completely missing from the traditions of Moses. Moses stands very close to God, but he is never called "God". Exodus 4: 16 comes very near to it, but it must be understood otherwise. And so it is with the Servant Songs. Probably this is connected with the "fiasco" of kingship, as Nyberg thinks; but we also know documents in the literature before the exile which are hostile or, at least, critical towards kingship. This explains the state of things in this respect in the traditions of Moses. Upon the whole, ancient Israel was often very dissatisfied with kingship. The absence of divine features in the picture of the Deutero-Isaianic "Messiah" I explain as a result of the anti-Canaanite reaction of the centuries before the exile.[4] We may speak of a "de-mythologizing" of the "Messianic picture" as well as of the religion of Israel in general. The chapter on the atoning suffering of the Innocent becomes a prefiguration of Good Friday and Easter Morning, but without the presuppositions of the Christmas Gospel of the Son of God.[5]

What is most remarkable, however, is the personal form of the "Messianic" preaching in these chapters. The Prophet has not only visualized the programme of vicarious suffering; he has seen it as a personal obligation. It has become his "Call", just as centuries later it became the "Call" of Jesus.

The prophet, like Jesus, emphasized the aspect of suffering. This "aspect" belongs also, as is continually and rightly stressed by Engnell, to the ancient king mythology; in our view, this is because it belongs to the myth of "First Man", which was the earlier prefiguration outside Israel of the description of the Sufferers in the Psalms and in Isaiah 49, 50, and 53. This is to be combined as well with Deutero-Isaiah's personal life. As the problem of unmerited suffering became *the* problem in the life of Jeremiah, so, too, it was the problem in the life of the Prophet of the Return. He saw its solution in the idea of vicarious suffering. Such was God's will (53: 10). The king of Israel became the Servant of all, making intercession for them as guilt offering and in prayer, in the figure of the new prophetic Moses.

Deutero-Isaiah and his Congregation of disciples saw their prophetic figure of the "Messiah" (although they never call him this) as their personal solution of the problem of suffering and as their personal task in the service of Israel, the world, and their neighbour, that is, in the service of God. Their "type"[6] was Moses of the Egyptian Exodus, who "carries the people as nurse" and risks his life for his people in intercession before the angry Divinity.

# 8

## THE ESCHATOLOGIZING AND
## RENAISSANCE OF THE MYTH

WE started our study with the Second Psalm. We saw that the Israelite king must be understood as a Saviour, actually present in the people assembled in the Sanctuary to repeat and "re-live" the great fundamental events of God's victory over the Powers of Evil. The king is a present "Messiah", no eschatological figure, but the sanctified, anointed, messenger of God. He guarantees the happiness of Israel in the New Year, inaugurated through the "remembrance" of God's saving acts of Creation. The "Messiah" of early Israel was not an "eschatological" figure, but the incarnation of God's blessing according to His covenant with Israel. But he did not remain so.

In the second volume of his *Psalmenstudien*, Mowinckel has shown that the historical experiences through which Israel had to pass led to "Eschatology".[1] Israel passed "from Experience to Hope". The realities of history did not confirm the faith, nourished by the experiences of the Enthronement Festival, that Israel's happiness was secured through the presence of the Anointed of Yahweh. The fall of both Israelite kingdoms in 721 and 587 necessarily made this discrepancy between faith and facts very keenly felt. Such is the background of the origin of "Eschatology".[2] Deutero-Isaiah worked in the faith and expectation of a "New" world-age, with a "New Myth". The Messianic bliss is not of this world; it will come with the New Creation. This New Creation is no longer connected with regularly returning days of the calendar. The festival no longer preaches "Salvation is here!" Rather, it keeps expectation alive—"Salvation *will come*! And it is very near."

The rise of Eschatology carries with it a new interpretation of the Enthronement Psalms. The Anointed of Yahweh is no longer a present figure. He is the coming king. This expectation is pre-exilic. Already before the exile, in the Royal Psalms of Isaiah 9, 11, and Micah 5, we find an "eschatologizing" of Royal Psalms.[3] Here Psalms like 72 are at work. The pattern of Psalm 2 we have met in Isaiah 42: 1ff.,[4] used in the description of Deutero-Isaiah's prophetic "Messiah". But there we do not find "eschatology". The Servant is still a present figure, a *Messias designatus*. The eschatologizing of Psalm 2 is encountered in the dream-vision of Daniel 7.

This prophetic "dream", in all its main features, follows the pattern of the psalm. First, we see the four terrible monsters rising out of the Sea. They correspond to the "kings of the earth" in the psalm, the instigators of the revolution against Yahweh and his Anointed. That the animals rise from the "Sea" and not, as in the psalm, from the "earth", is irrelevant. The "Sea" and the "Earth" are symbols of the same idea, the powers hostile to God, the "Chaos". Nevertheless, this change of expression has some significance. The "kings of the earth" in the psalm were characterized as being only terrestrial. That the eschatological monsters come from the sea expresses their demonic character more strongly. The vision of the apocalyptist is more "mythological" than the psalm, not only by mentioning the "Sea", the great Enemy of the Creator, but also in describing the "kings of the earth" as horrible monsters. The psalm is probably influenced by the tendency to that "historification" which was peculiar to Israel. In Daniel's dream, we observe what we may call the *Renaissance of Mythology* in later Judaism. While the anti-Canaanite reaction of pre-exilic days led to a "de-mythologizing" of the "Messiah" and of the Creation festival, later Judaism seems to have accepted this material again to a great extent. It had now passed through the purgatory of Israel's history. Monotheism was now so firmly rooted that mythology could not imperil Israel's religion. Therefore, in this respect the dream of Daniel is more "antique" than the psalm, the pattern of which is the pattern of the dream.

As in the psalm, the noisy upheaval of the Human Empires, represented by the fabulous animals, is contrasted with a picture of sublime calmness. "The Ancient of Days" judges the monsters. As the culmination of the revelation, there appears the *"Son of Man"*, the incarnation of the *Kingdom of God*. This corresponds to the proclamation of the king in Psalm 2. That the Son of Man is described as identical with the kingdom of God, with God's people, is no matter of difficulty. The Royal Messiah of the ancient cult was also identical with God's people, and in writings which take no special interest in the personal Messiah, but concentrate on the kingdom of God, this feature tends to vanish into the background. To the people of God, described as the Son of Man, world dominion is given that God may reign for eternity. The animals are annihilated. The judgment, still only a possibility in the psalm, is now seen as executed.

As I have said in my commentary on Daniel, the vision of chapter 7 is an eschatologized representation of the ancient Enthronement Festival. It has been influenced by the idea of world periods, peculiar to eschatology proper. It culminates in the taking over of world dominion by the Jewish people, represented by the figure of the "Son of Man".[5]

Later Jewish theologians (and the ecclesiastical exegetes who followed them) had no idea of the real, original meaning of the "cultic pattern" of the Near East. The result of the anti-Canaanite reaction of Israel was that it could be used without detriment to new religion, as a description of the Age to Come. Daniel 7—as everybody knows—is not the only place where traditional material appears.[6] The later eschatological "Messianic" interpretation, which in many respects rests on *typology*, is to a great extent a return in refined forms to the conception of the king as identical with the Son of God, in Canaan with Ba'al himself. For the sake of refinement, Ba'al had to be expelled from Israel's world of thought, but the idea that the Saviour was not only of Israel, but also from "Heaven", from the Higher World, the World of Divinity, "the durative world" (as Gaster puts it), had been outlined by the Ancient East. In Israel, the idea was preserved by borrowing the notion of adoption, also found, e.g. in Mesopotamia. The New Testament again speaks of a Prince "born of a woman", but also *"ante omnia saecula"*, and so it is linked up with the king mythology of the Ancient East.[7]

The Second Psalm cannot be interpreted as dealing directly with *Jesus* the Christ, but its conception of the Messiah, as an "eschatologizing" of the Saviour of the ancient rituals, certainly establishes a close connection between the psalm and the "Fulfilment". When we speak of "Fulfilment", we are using— as we said before—an interpretation of faith. But to draw the "Messianic Line", as we have attempted here, is to furnish this interpretation of faith with a very valuable foundation in the phenomenology of religion. The King Messiah of Psalm 2 is a "prefiguration", a *typos*, of the eschatological Messiah, of the Son of Man in later Judaism and the New Testament. That the Son of Man, Primeval Man, and Messiah have common roots has been said before. In this way, the "Anointed" of Psalm 2 becomes a "pre-figuration" of the Christ of the Church.[8]

But this process was not completed without important additions. In this interpretation of the Messiah of the Psalms, what is called by Engnell the "Aspect of Suffering" was pre-eminently drawn into the foreground. Isaiah 53 acquired a decisive importance.[9] But we have seen that this chapter, too, had its lines of connection with the ancient ideology of the Primeval Man and King. The Fulfilment assumes features which had been rejected by the anti-Canaanite reaction of Israel. Even the idea of death and resurrection of the divine saviour has been placed in the centre of the New Testament world of thought, while the Old Testament type (Isaiah 53) had expurgated the divine features completely. The expurgation had been a sort of disintegration of the original pattern. The Fulfilment re-integrates the lost but necessary range of ideas to suggest that humanity alone cannot save humanity. The Saviour must come from Above. This thought had been lost through the reaction against "heathenism"; but the "heathen" truth had to be recovered.

Thus it is that religio-historical research serves Theology. I had almost said that the History of Religions and the Interpretation of Faith confirm one another.

Nevertheless, one must not slur over the difference between Prefiguration and Fulfilment. It is an inherent principle of typology that the Antitype is always greater, and often in opposition to, the Type.[10] For example, Psalm 2, as it stands, is the expression of a totalitarian political claim which must be rejected in favour of the pure totalitarian claims of the Kingdom of God. Regenerated on the higher level of the Gospel, the political totalitarian claim of the psalm can be regarded as a "presentiment" of the conviction that only under the rule of the Son, sent by God, the *homoousios tô patri*, can there be security for the nations of this world.

We have seen that the conception of the Messiah is presented to us in three forms with common roots—three aspects of a totality which in different ages have been accentuated in different ways.

First, we described the *Royal Messiah* of the Ancient Nations and of pre-exilic Israel, as he is presented by the Royal Psalms. He is the fighter in the ritual combat of the Creation Drama, the Bearer of Salvation, present in full actuality in the "re-living" of the saving facts in the New Year Festival. He has suffered the vicissitudes of the combat, but is now able to proclaim the victory of God.

Secondly, we considered the *Moses redivivus*, described as the Prophet of the Exile who, in the shape of the Innocent Sufferer, secures the Salvation of the people.

And finally, we considered the Heavenly *Son of Man*, as the impersonation of the Kingdom of God in the Book of Daniel.

These types, however, are not successive phases in a history, in which they appear one after another as absolute *nova*. They all have features common to what the Uppsala scholars call "king ideology". In the first type, we meet the Victor; in the second, the Suffering Servant; and in the third, the transcendence of the Son of Man is accentuated.

We have seen that we ought perhaps to regard the idea of "First Man" (rather than the king ideology) as the connecting element between the three types. The First King and the First Prophet are both "aspects" of the same type, the Saviour and First Ancestor, the Patriarch, conceived differently, with different emphases on the various elements in different circles. The final picture, the Son of Man, seems to give the best expression of the entire type. Different ages accentuated different aspects: the ancient age, the king; the school of Deutero-Isaiah, the suffering First Prophet. That the latter is described as *Moses redivivus* is due to several factors, but,

above all, to historical circumstances. Israel was living in a
time which was analogous to the Exodus-situation, and when,
in prophetic and deuteronomistic circles, Moses had become
the normative type of a prophet. The strong transcendence of
the Son of Man is also traceable to the circumstances of the
time. The Hellenistic period had strongly transcendentalized
the idea of God. Accordingly, the Divine King had to follow
the lead. The Book of Daniel stresses the sole activity of God
in Salvation, and so the heavenly and not the "individual"
character of the Saviour is emphasized.

But all three types of the Saviour have common roots. If we
wish to speak of "evolution" in this connection, we should
have to mean a process which, through the centuries, altern-
ately brings to the fore different components of the type as
dominating features in the picture of the Messiah. Whether
that can properly be called "evolution", I leave to the
biologists.

These different components are all present in the Psalm
Literature. This Literature was our starting point, since king
ideology and everything else (including the First Man ideology) is present there. The expression "Son of Man" has been
found in the Psalms, as well as the theology of Suffering.
Here the central position of the Psalms in the literature of
the Old Testament becomes obvious. An Old Testament
Theology could very appropriately start with a description of
the religion of the Psalter.

Further, we must stress that the roots of the Messianic ideas
are found outside the Old Testament. The theological consequences of this must be taken into account by students of Dogmatics and Ethics more positively than, I think, is commonly
done. Of course, the differences between the king ideology and
Messianism of the Ancient East and that of the Old Testament
will have to be fully appreciated. In this connection, the
position taken about the question of "Mythology" which
reveals itself in different ages is important.

In the period of the Israelite Monarchy, we encounter, in the
anti-Canaanite reaction, a tendency towards "de-mythologizing". The death of the Divine King is not accepted as an
"article of faith" in Israel, but expressions originating in this

circle of ideas have been retained in cultic poetry. Even the idea of the divinity of kings was taken over, but it was adapted to Israelite conceptions. The notion of Divine Sonship by adoption, known from Mesopotamia, was probably the form in which divine kingship could be tolerated. Later, in Deutero-Isaiah, every trace of it vanished.

However, in later Judaism and in the Early Church we observe a "renaissance of mythology". The ancient conceptions of the Divine King were used as material in Christian circles for the development of a Christology as early as the New Testament. Here the rôle played by the "aspect of suffering" from Isaiah 53, which is combined with the figure of the Son of Man, is of first importance. The result is that Jesus re-unites all aspects of the idea of Primeval Man and Primeval King in His own person, and so the entire mythology of the Ancient East is re-instated.

Systematic Theology must learn from both these currents. It is necessary to appreciate both the criticism springing from the anti-Canaanite reaction and also the positive attitude of the mythological renaissance in later Judaism and the Early Church.[11]

We may conclude with some final observations concerning this "renaissance of mythology".

We have said that Israel travelled the road "from experience to hope". The present Messiah was changed into the eschatological Messiah under the pressure of the realities of history—the defeats, decline and fall of the kingdom and of the nation as an independent political entity.

But we find still another change, when we pursue the line further into the Church and its world of faith. The Kingdom of God in the preaching of the Gospel is not only, as in Judaism, the Coming Kingdom. In certain words of Jesus, and in the sacramental conception of the New Testament as a whole, the kingdom is present in Jesus himself, both in his historical appearance and in his Body the Church. It is this *"hodie"* which is so impressively stressed by Daniélou and characterized as the specifically Christian idea in eschatology. This means that, with Christ and His Church, the idea of the present Messiah has returned and again become a vital force in religion. We find also a "renaissance" of the ideology in the ancient cult. In the Church, in the *Corpus Christi*, the King and Saviour is really present—as expressed in the communion hymn of Grundtvig alluded to at the outset of this study. In the cultic experience of the Church, both in the Roman Mass and the Protestant service, as also in the preaching and in the individual reading of the Bible, the Messiah is present, bringing with him Salvation from God. A significant historical cycle was completed when the ideology of ancient rituals was utilized by the first Christians to express their meeting with Jesus of Nazareth and the effects on them of His personality. It was this which created the "New Myth" visualized by Deutero-Isaiah, now the "antitype" of the "types" in the Old Testament, the Exodus from Egypt and from Babylon.

# ABBREVIATIONS USED IN THE NOTES

| | |
|---|---|
| B.J.R.L. | *Bulletin of the John Rylands Library* |
| D.T.T. | *Dansk Teologisk Tidsskrift* |
| E.T. | *Expository Times* |
| E.VV. | *English Versions* |
| G.T.M.M.M. | *Det Gamle Testament, oversatt av S. Michelet, S. Mowinckel og N. Messel* |
| H.T.R. | *Harvard Theological Review* |
| I.R. | *Illustreret Religionsleksikon* |
| J.A.O.S. | *Journal of the American Oriental Society* |
| J.B.L. | *Journal of Biblical Literature* |
| J.N.E.S. | *Journal of Near Eastern Studies* |
| J.S.O.R. | *Journal of the Society for Oriental Research* |
| M.A.O.G. | *Mitteilungen der altorientalischen Gesellschaft* |
| N.T.T. | *Norsk Teologisk Tidsskrift* |
| O.T.S. | *Oudtestamentische Studiën* |
| R.B. | *Revue Biblique* |
| R.Bib. | *Religion och Bibel* |
| R.H.P.R. | *Revue d'Histoire et de Philosophie religieuses* |
| S.E.Å. | *Svensk Exegetisk Årsbok* |
| S.J.T. | *Scottish Journal of Theology* |
| S.T. | *Studia Theologica* |
| S.T.K. | *Svensk Teologisk Kvartalskrift* |
| T.R. | *Theologische Rundschau* |

F

| | |
|---|---|
| T.T. | *Theologisk Tidsskrift* |
| U.U.Å. | *Uppsala Universitets Årsskrift* |
| W.Z.K.M. | *Wiener Zeitschrift für die Kunde des Morgenlandes* |
| Z.A.W. | *Zeitschrift für die alttestamentliche Wissenschaft* |
| Z.D.M.G. | *Zeitschrift der deutschen morgenländischen Gesell-schaft* |

# NOTES

*N.B.*—*Owing to the author's death, it has not been possible to check all the references to other books as given in the Notes.*

## Chapter 1

1. For a survey, see A. R. Johnson, in *The Old Testament and Modern Study* (1951); cf. his observations in *E.T.*, LXII (1950), pp. 36ff.

2. The movement has not affected the Western World as much as the Scandinavian countries, where Mowinckel's influence has been most penetrating.

3. To understand the Scandinavian approach, it is necessary to be acquainted with the view of this extremely influential thinker. His *magnum opus*, *Vor folkeaet i oldtiden I–IV* (1909–12) is available for English readers in the translation, *The Culture of the Teutons*, I–III (1930–31). His essay on *Ritual Drama* (English edition, vol. II, pp. 26off.) is of great importance for our present study. Very similar ideas are expressed by Th. Gaster, *Thespis* (1950).

4. The interpretation of these psalms in Mowinckel's *Psalmenstudien II* (1922) has never been radically refuted; cf. my observations in *S.T.*, III, 2 (1949) (Lund, 1951), pp. 154ff. It is the principle of the "Gattungsforschung" which (to mention an example from the history of Hellenistic literature) is so admirably applied by Festugière to the texts of the Corpus Hermeticum (*Les Révélations d'Hermès Trismégiste*, II, 1949, pp. 9ff., 28ff.). But the "Gattungsforschung" is only time-honoured philological method adapted to the Oriental literary situation.

5. Ps. 96: 5 (Moffatt).

6. cf. N. A. Dahl, *Anamnesis*, in *S.T.*, I, 1–2, 1947 (Lund, 1948), pp. 69ff.

7. The "typological exegesis" of the N.T. and the early Church cannot be accepted as "historical exegesis", since it presupposes an interpretation of history based on Jesus as the fulfilment for religious faith. But it can be an important theological addition to historical interpretation, when it is adapted to our historical mode of thinking. In its own time, it was *historical* interpretation and our adaptation is a consequence of this fact; cf. Goppelt, *Typos* (1939); Daniélou, *Sacramentum Futuri* (1950) and my review of the latter in *Erasmus* (1951), pp. 213ff. On the subject of the principle of interpretation, see Goppelt, *op. cit.*, p. 195 and below, ch. VIII, note 8.

8. I shall not enlarge on the much-discussed theory of the "ritual pattern". The Uppsala scholars have made it clear that the "pattern" itself does not exist, but is a presumption, like an "ursemitisch" language. But the similarity of the New Year Festivals is an established fact and poses a problem which has to be accepted and dealt with. Frankfort's way of dealing with the Psalms (*The Problem of Similarity in Ancient Near Eastern Religions*,

1951, p. 8) exhibits the same ignorance of Hebrew problems as his Epilogue to *Kingship and the Gods*, and makes it difficult to take up a discussion with him at the level of O.T. scholarship. The Ancient Near East to which Israel belongs was a cultural unity with many shades and variations, like our own Western European culture. As part of this unity, we must reckon its cultic forms, which (as Widengren has shown) are much more alike than Gunkel and his disciples thought. But there are also many variations within this wealth of forms and similar features may have different meanings in the different "provinces" of the cultural area. The significance of such "difference-in-similarity" is most lucidly set forth by H. Birkeland in his article on "The Belief in the Resurrection of the Dead in the Old Testament", *S.T.*, III, 1, 1949 (Lund, 1950).

9. Here I refer to the remarks of Lindblom on "method" in the *Bertholet-Festschrift* (1948).

10. *Weeping and Laughter in the Old Testament: a Study of Israelite Religion*, (Leiden and Köbenhavn, 1962); cf. his description of Canaanite religion in his *Den israelitiske Religions Historie* (Copenhagen, 1943).

11. See the symposia *Myth and Ritual* (1933) and *The Labyrinth* (1935), edited by S. H. Hooke and the Schweich Lectures of the same scholar, *The Origins of Early Semitic Ritual* (1938). The Uppsala School joined the debate with the "Myth and Ritual School" with Ivan Engnell's *Studies in Divine Kingship in the Ancient Near East* (1943) and his investigations of the Karit text from Ras Shamra, "The Text K II from Ras Shamra" (in *R. Bib.*, Nathan Söderblomsällskapets Årsbok, 1944, pp. 1ff.). The discussion was continued by G. Widengren's article, "Det sakrala kungadömet bland öst-och västsemiter", *R. Bib.*, 1943, pp. 49ff. An admirable survey of the ideas of this school is given by G. W. Anderson in his paper, "Some Aspects of the Uppsala School of Old Testament Study" (*H.T.R.*, XLIII, 1950, pp. 239ff.). There is an equally sober appreciation by A. R. Johnson, in *E.T.*, LXII (1950), pp. 36ff. I may also refer to my own survey in *T.R.* (1948–49), pp. 317ff. and my discussion of special points in the volumes presented to Lindblom (*S.E.Å.*, 1947) and to Eissfeldt (1947). Mowinckel has criticized the work of Engnell and Widengren in *N.T.T.* (1944), pp. 70ff. and certain points in the Swiss edition of the present book in *S.T.* (1948) (cf. my reply in the same journal in 1951). He has repeated his criticism in his great book, *He That Cometh* (Oxford, 1956), and I shall return to these questions below.

For the background of the whole discussion, reference must be made to Johs. Pedersen's *Israel, its Life and Culture*, I–IV (1926–40); "Canaanite and Israelite Cultus" (*Acta Orientalia*, 1940, pp. 1ff.); and "Die Krt-Legende", in *Berytus*, ed. Ingholt, VI (1941), pp. 63ff. See also H. S. Nyberg, "Smärtornas Man", *S.E.Å.*, 1942, and his short essay on *Hosea-boken* in *U.U.Å.*, 1941.

In addition to the chief works already mentioned, reference should be made to Widengren's interesting article in *Horae Soederblomianae*, I, *Mélanges Johs. Pedersen* (1947), in which he studies some texts from pseudepigraphic literature and a piece of the Samaritan liturgy: "Till det sakrala kunga-dömets historia i Israel, (i) Den himmelska intronisationen i judisk-hellenistisk tid; (ii) Konungen i lövhyddofestens ritual". The two chapters show that the ideas from the Ancient Royal Ritual live on in late texts.

On the subject of the "anamnesis" of the facts of Salvation, I must refer to Johs. Pedersen, *Israel*, III–IV, pp. 401ff.; 408ff. on the Passover-ritual; also van der Leeuw, *Phänomenologie der Religion* (1933), p. 344. In this connection, I may perhaps be allowed to add a personal note. One of my fundamental experiences was in a conversation with some friends, when one of them interpreted the Communion pericope of St. Luke's Gospel. The situation suddenly became a reality to me. Such things happen everywhere, when the Holy Spirit actualizes the word of the Bible and the congregation becomes contemporaneous with Christ. Phenomenologically, the cultic experience of the Ancient Easterners is the same, in the O.T. as well as in the non-biblical religions. The decisive difference must be placed in the "objective factor", in the Divine Word which is met with in the ritual. Is it the true God or an idol? Here, the decisive factor is the principle of what Luther called "Christum treiben", cf. 1 Cor. 12: 1–3. I make no special claims for my own experience and I mention it only to emphasize the fact that it is important to keep in mind that the ancient cults are not mere antiquities, but daily realities in the lives of men. Religion is a living fact to-day; the world ought to know that, and above all its scholars.—The Christian experience is described in beautiful French by Festugière in *La Sainteté* (1942), pp. 69f.

In principle, I accept the view of the Swedish scholars that the Psalms have been influenced by the royal ritual (cf. my *Det sakrale kongedömme*, 1945). I am critical of the tendency to overlook nuances and make premature generalizations; and I am conscious of the danger of forgetting that, when the Israelite Psalms were composed, the period during which psalms were used in the royal ritual both in Babylon and Israel was long past. I may add that I do not like the superficial way in which literary criticism is dismissed with such slogans as "evolutionism" and "logicism" by some of the Swedish scholars. The significance of the Uppsala School lies in its synthesis of earlier Scandinavian and Anglo-American scholarship—a work which was necessary and which has been carried out with great acumen and learning. Engnell, especially, has made important contributions to the interpretation of the Ras Shamra texts.

The Scandinavian School has, indeed, met with some important opposition. See, for example, the article by A. Alt, "The Monarchy in the Kingdoms of Israel and Judah", in *Essays on Old Testament History and Religion* (Oxford, 1966), pp. 241 ff. and Noth's "God, King, and Nation in the Old Testament", in *The Laws in the Pentateuch and Other Essays* (Edinburgh, 1966), pp. 145ff.

Although I do not completely disagree with these two scholars, when Noth denies every kind of "divinity" in the Israelite conception of kingship *(op. cit.,* pp. 174f.), I am bound to say that I believe he is misinterpreting his material. It is quite mistaken to call Ps. 45: 7 "unique" in the whole of the O.T. and his concession about Ps. 2: 7 (on page 172) is enough to invalidate his position. Further, when the Messiah is certainly described as a "sacral" or "divine" king in Isa. 9 and 11 and Micah 5, and when formulae like Isa. 7: 14 (with its Ugaritic counterpart) are used in Jerusalemitic royal etiquette, it cannot be denied that the kings—whose ancestor became the type of the Messiah—were invested with divine qualities. The truth in the contention of Noth and Alt is to be found in what I call the "anti-Canaanite reaction", which in the course of time led to a "demythologizing" of the idea of the king. The basis of their criticism is the views about the Psalms which they share with many contemporary scholars. It is the inability of Gunkel to see the importance of Mowinckel's work which stands in the way of German progress in this field.—See also the popular but well-documented Norwegian work, *Keiseren på Himmeltronen* (1949), by H. P. L'Orange.—On the book of Kraus, *Die Königsherrschaft Gottes im Alten Testament* (1951), I defer my judgment.

12. It is curious how the "typological interpretation" of the Church here is a return to the ancient creation ideology (cf. Daniélou, *op. cit.*, pp. 155ff.). See below, p. 110, n. 8.

## Chapter 2

1. cf. Meissner, *Babylonien und Assyrien*, p. 65; Kees, *Ägypten* (1933), p. 177; and Frankfort, *Kingship and the Gods* (1948).

1a. cf. further Thiele, *The Mysterious Numbers of the Hebrew Kings* (1951), ch. II.

2. In connection with the polemics against this idea, found for example in Gordon's *Ugaritic Literature*, see the review by Ginsberg in *J.A.O.S.*, 70 (1950), p. 157. I want to see more serious arguments, before I consider the position taken in Hvidberg's book shaken (see above, p. 13). The repetition cannot be denied by arguments like the reference to the fact that Ba'al's death and resurrection is recounted only once in the Ras Shamra mythological texts. It would be as easy to argue that the "hapax" of Heb. 9: 25ff. proves that the Roman Church does not teach the repetition of the sacrifice of Christ in the Mass. The rest of the arguments are of the same kind. As Ginsberg suggests, there is something to be said for the annual reading of certain holy texts. The texts and rites have developed along separate lines; cf. Frankfort's *The Problem of Similarity* (1951), p. 10, where he does not deny the re-enacting of the primeval events in the ritual, not even in Israel (p. 8, n. 1).

3. On the idea of the Patriarch, see Nyberg's important treatment in *Hoseaboken*, in *U.U.Å.* (1941). Among the Semites, the patriarch was the divine ancestor of the tribe who lives and is incorporated in it. Of course,

this idea was modified by the Israelite conception of God, but it underlies the idea of the patriarchs—both of mankind and the tribes; cf. below, pp. 45ff.

4. cf. the texts quoted by Labat in *Le Caractère religieux de la Royauté assyro-babylonienne* (1939), pp. 40–52. There is a discussion on this subject between Mowinckel and myself in *S.T.*, II, 1 (1948–49). It also deals with the following section of this book on the "First Man", the patriarch of mankind as first king. I am not convinced by Mowinckel's arguments and so for the most part my treatment remains as it was in the Swiss edition.

On the ideas of divine rulers in later periods, see Festugière, in *Histoire Générale des Religions*, ed. Gorce and Mortier, Grèce-Rome (1947), pp. 127ff.; Festugière and Fabre, *Le Monde Gréco-Romain au temps de notre Seigneur*, I–II (1935), II, pp. 7ff.; Prümm, *Religionsgeschichtliches Handbuch für den Raum der altchristlichen Umwelt*, 1943, pp. 54ff.; and H. P. L'Orange, *Keiseren på Himmeltronen* (Oslo, 1949).

4a. cf. also Isa. 9: 1–2, and Dodd, *According to the Scriptures* (1952), p. 80.

5. cf. *S.T.*, III, 2, 1949 (Lund, 1951), pp. 151f.

6. For the reading of the corrupt verse, see my commentary and Widengren's important article, "Psalm 110 och det sakrala kungadömet i Israel", in *U.U.Å.* (1941), 7. 1. It is significant that we have arrived independently at virtually the same reconstruction of the text, which I translate: "With thee is royal power on the day of thy strength. On holy mountains I have begotten thee, from the womb of woman, before the morning star and the dew". Widengren translates: "Thy people is coming as volunteers on the day of thy strength. In holy array step forth from the womb of Dawn, as Day I have begotten thee" (cf. below, p. 88, n. 16).

7. *R. Bib.* (1943), p. 59, n. 1.

8. "Opphavet til den senjödiske forestilling om Menneskesönnen", in *N.T.T.* (1944), p. 197; cf. my *Det sakrale kongedömme*, pp. 116f. and *S.T.*, III, 2, 1949 (Lund, 1951) p. 148.

8a. It should be noted that expressions like "my holy mountain" seem to be common Canaanite phrases, cf. Virolleaud, *La déesse Anat*, p. 41 (*V AB.*, c. 27–28). I hope to return to this significant fact in another connection.

9. cf. my article in the Lindblom volume of *S.E.Å.* (1947), pp. 44ff., and again *S.T.*, III, 2, p. 153.

10. On this element of prophetic style, see my *Introduction to the Old Testament*, I, pp. 196ff.

11. It is also worth noting that *'âz* is used in the morning prayer of the synagogue expressly to denote Yahweh's work as Creator, in the prayer *hammê'îr lâ 'âreṣ*. Here we read, *hammelek hammᵉrômâm lᵉbaddô mê'âz* in parallel with *mîmôt-'ôlâm*, and God is called "king".

12. This is an idea of predestination like that described in Labat's *Le Caractère religieux de la Royauté assyro-babylonienne*. The meaning of the word in the ritual, however, is that this is now fulfilled, or better, re-experienced, repeated.

13. cf. Engnell, *Studies*, in the Topical Index, under "Divinator". This feature of the psalm—the fact that the king himself proclaims the oracle of Yahweh, that is, that he acts as prophet—is very significant. The king has the chief right to receive oracles because kings are the nearest to the divine world. Cf. further, Boll, *Aus der Offenbarung des Johannes* (Stoicheia, I (1914), pp. 136ff.); Festugière, *Les Révélations d'Hermès Trismégiste*, I (1944), pp. 324ff. The Egyptian ideas of the Divine King still live on in the hermetic literature. Here the king is the "last of the gods" and "the first of men".

14. On the not very precise meaning of this term in Mesopotamia, see Labat, *op. cit.*, pp. 54ff., 58. Sometimes, we get the impression that the king was *created* by the goddess, as the First Man was created. But other texts refer the creation indicated here to the embryonic life of the king in his mother's womb. It may be that we have a parallel to the O.T., where it is said that Man is formed in the depths of the Earth, but also (in the same context) that the formation takes place in the mother's womb (Ps. 139: 13–15; cf. Job 1: 21); cf. Mowinckel, "Moder Jord i det Gamle Testamente" in *Studier tillägnade Edv. Lehmann* (1927). But I suppose that the relationship between the "earth" and the "womb" is the same as that between "tomb" and "Sheol", as described by Johs. Pedersen in *Israel I–II* and as that between "Heaven" and "Sanctuary" in (for example) Ps. 20. A similar parallelism would explain the imprecise presentation of the Divine Sonship of Mesopotamian kings: "creation" and "being formed in the womb of the mother" are identical phenomena.

15. "Adoption" is generally understood as a milder, more "demythologized", expression of Divine Sonship than so-called "physical" sonship. I do not think it is. As described by Labat, that is, as a sort of "milk-relationship", it must have been just as "physical" as "real" sonship. Nevertheless, the facts show that Divine Kingship in Mesopotamia is conceived in more subordinationist terms than in Egypt, where the king is really a god.

16. As I said above (p. 87, n. 6), I think that Ps. 110: 3 originally described the supernatural birth of the king in more mythological terms. The usual translation is based on a number of presuppositions (and in some cases unjustifiable). The Hebrew *yaldûth* probably should not be translated "youth", meaning "young warriors", but in the abstract sense of "youthful strength" (cf. Eccles. 11: 9f.), *b^ehadrê kôdeš*, which is rendered "in holy array" (cf. Ps. 29: 2; 2 Chron. 20: 21), perhaps signifying the priestly costume, is not a good expression for the holiness of the army, which, according to the context, must be the theme of the verse. The reading *b^ehar^erê kôdeš* (cf. Ps. 87: 1) is well attested. The idea of "dew from the womb of dawn" is not clear (to put it mildly) and is not explained by

Isa. 26: 19. The form *mišḥâr*, which occurs only here, is also doubtful. The ancient versions show a text which, in spite of some obscure expressions, is at least more intelligible in places. This text has some very "mythological" terms (cf. Vulg.: "tecum principium in die virtutis tuae in splendoribus sanctorum: ex utero ante luciferum genui te"; LXX gives the same idea). Neither has accounted for the enigmatic words *lᵉkâ ṭal*, which seem to have been read by the Syriac version. This Syriac reading may be explained by the observations of J. Jeremias in *Theol. Wörterbuch zum Neuen Testament*, I: 343: 9ff., quoted by Goppelt, *Typos*, p. 228, that *ṭalyâ delâhâ* is the equivalent of *'Ebed Yahwe*. The Syriac understood our Hebrew text (*ṭal*) as the Aramaic *ṭalyâ*, meaning "servant". But originally, there may have been a reference to a goddess of the dew, known from Ras Shamra (II AB 1: 10ff. 4: 50ff. I AB 5: 10ff.; V AB 1: 22ff.; V ABC 3ff.; cf. Aistleitner in *Z.D.M.G.*, 1939, p. 55), mentioned here in parallel with *šaḥar*, Lucifer, the god of the morning star. *reḥem* could mean "woman" (as in Judg. 5: 30; *Mesha Inscription*, line 17), here the divine mother of the king (cf. Gal. 4: 4: *genomenos ek gunaikos*). As was said above, Widengren reads a similar text; cf. also Mowinckel, *Kongesalmerne* (1916), p. 30; *He That Cometh* (1956), p. 75, and n. 4 (with references to Widengren and Engnell), and also pp. 62, 67, 103, 117, with accompanying notes. See further, Hammershaimb, *Some Aspects of Israelite Prophecy* (Köbenhavn, 1966), pp. 9–16; Nyberg, *I.R.*, II, pp. 234–37. Of course, the reconstruction of the corrupt verse must be used with every caution. I note that in my commentary I overlooked the similar interpretation of the text given by A. R. Johnson in *The Labyrinth*, ed. Hooke (1935), p. 110.

16a. cf. 1 Sam. 10: 6b, 9a, E. J. Young, *My Servants the Prophets* (1952), pp. 86f.

17. cf. Hildegard Lewy in *Symbolae ad studia orientis pertinentes Frederico Hrozný dedicatae II* (Prague, 1949—Archiv Orientální, XVII), pp. 86ff.

18. On ritual oracles, see further Mowinckel, *Psalmenstudien*, III (1923).

19. This interpretation of Ps. 2 has also been questioned by Mowinckel in an article in *S.T.*, II, 1 (1949), pp. 88ff. I have replied in *S.T.*, III, 2 (1951), pp. 150 and 153 (where the reference on p. 153 to p. 8 should be to p. 150). I agree, of course, with Mowinckel that the enthronement of the king is an event of the present day, but I cannot see that he is criticizing my idea when he adds that it is the experience of the re-creation of the "primordial time" in the sacramental "Here and Now" of the festival. That is exactly what I mean and what, I think, Johs. Pedersen, to whom I referred, means. It is this conception which I apply to the "to-day" of the psalm. When Mowinckel goes on to say that Ps. 89: 20 refers to an historical situation, with some reservations, again I agree. I think, however, that Mowinckel forgets that the election of the house of David, which to us is *only* an historical event, is more to Israel. Like the Exodus, it is an event of primordial character, repeated, "re-lived" (as Johs. Pedersen says) in the enthronement of every new "David" on the throne of Yahweh in Jerusalem (cf. Ps. 99: 6). When Mowinckel questions my interpretation of Ps. 2 as

an "historification" of the "chaos"—or "fight of the nations" myth, and
in this connection refers to Pss. 46, 28 and 76 and Zech. 14, I can only ask
readers to have an unprejudiced look at those texts. Some years ago, I was
quite suddenly struck by the close formal similarity between Pss. 2 and 46.
The chief difference is that the king is not mentioned in Ps. 46. But the
"nations" are there, in strophes 2 and 3, and in close parallelism to the
"waters", i.e. the "Chaos" in the first strophe. Here we have the "historifying" identification of the "waters" of the primeval flood and the *gôyîm*.
The enemies of Ps. 46: 6 are the chaos powers of v. 3, and consequently of
Ps. 2, which are "actualized" in the "nations". The "actual political
situation" at the accession of a new king is viewed as the threatening
outbreak of the "flood".

## Chapter 3

1. This is rightly stressed by Frankfort in his Frazer Lecture on *The
Problem of Similarity*. He is also right in emphasizing the supreme importance of the differences. These are the factors which determine the independent value of the concrete "pattern" in question. Its individual qualities
are the clue to the interpretation of the similarities and so we can never
start our investigations of (say) Israelite conceptions in Babylon. This
principle is stressed by Lindblom in the *Bertholet-Festschrift* and by Johs.
Pedersen (see the quotations from *Israel*, I–II (Danish edition, 1934) given
in my review of Scandinavian literature in *T.R.* (1948–49), pp. 276–77).
Nevertheless, when we start with the Israelite material, parallels may be
used inside the cultural area of the Ancient Near East with the same confidence as that shown by Frankfort in using features from African tribes to
elucidate Egyptian kingship. The close relationship between the Oriental
cultures is rightly stressed by Mowinckel in *He That Cometh* (1956), pp. 23ff.,
but see also the words of Engnell quoted below, p. 55.

2. See further my criticism of Vriezen's brief attack on Mowinckel's
position in his interesting *Hoofdlijnen der Theologie van het Oude Testament*
(1949) in *S.T.*, III, 2, pp. 154f. It applies also to Snaith's work, *The Jewish
New Year Festival* (1947).

3. *J.A.O.S.* 70 (1950), p. 157. This is not reading the texts to find a "mean-
ing-behind-the-meaning"; on the contrary, it is to take the text seriously.
It may also be noted that the distinction of Frankfort (*The Problem of
Similarity*, p. 8) between "poetic expression of religious feeling" and "distinct
reference to rites" in the psalms is mistaken. It is the same error which
made his Epilogue to *Kingship and the Gods*, "a mere trifling with the question
at issue" which "mars what is otherwise a most stimulating and important
piece of work" (A. R. Johnson in the *Book List* of the British Society for Old
Testament Study, 1948). The work of Hans Schmidt, which Frankfort

praises, uses the same form-critical method as Mowinckel. The psalms are *both* a "poetic expression of religious feeling" *and* allusions to the cultic situations in which these feelings were expressed.

4. cf. above, p. 83, n. 4.

5. *Psalm 110 im Lichte der neueren altorientalischen Forschung*, in the *Vorlesungsverzeichnis der Staatl. Akademie in Braunsberg für das Wintersemester* (1929–30).

6. *Psalmenstudien*, III, pp. 82f.

7. See Labat, *Le Caractère religieux*, pp. 82ff.

8. These Egyptian plays are described in detail by Frankfort in *Kingship and the Gods*. He also gives good descriptions of the Assyrian rites, but (as I noted in my article in *S.T.*, III, 2, pp. 144ff.) he seems to overrate the differences between Egypt and Mesopotamia. These differences cannot be denied, but it is erroneous to reduce too much the divine status of the Assyrian king.

9. cf. Hvidberg's description of the Ras Shamra "myths" as the "programme of the play" (words of Grönbech) in *Weeping and Laughter in the Old Testament* (1962), pp. 52f. with reference to Grönbech and Gaster. It is to these pages that Ginsberg alludes in so unsatisfactory a manner (cf. p. 22). Readers are asked to read Grönbech, before they let such facile words determine their opinion (cf. above, p. 11).

10. cf. above, p. 87, n. 6.

11. See the remarks on methodology above, p. 12.

12. *Myth and Ritual* (1933), pp. 7f.; cf. Frankfort, *The Problem of Similarity*, p. 9.

13. See my review of Frankfort's book in *D.T.T.* (1949) and *S.T.*, III, 2, 1949 (Lund, 1951), pp. 143ff., especially p. 147.

14. cf. Gadd, *Ideas of Divine Rule in the Ancient East* (1948), pp. 47f.: "it may be said that the result is to find divinity constantly implied, seldom averred". See also Thorkild Jacobsen's description of the identification of kings with gods in the sacred marriage rite, *The Intellectual Adventure of Ancient Man*, by Frankfort, Wilson, Jacobsen and Irwin (1948), pp. 198f., and especially p. 200: "To the very end of Mesopotamian Civilization, a few centuries before our era, the king, every new year in Babylon, took on the identity of Marduk and vanquished Kingu, leader of Tiamat's host, by burning a lamb in which that deity was incarnate".—Cf. Labat, *Le Caractère religieux*, pp. 164, 234ff., 240–45; and also p. 184.

15. For the Israelite conception, see below, pp. 26ff.

16. cf. my *Det sakrale kongedömme*, pp. 65ff. and Engnell, *Studies*, p. 142, n. 1.

17. cf. my *Det sakrale kongedömme*, pp. 77ff.

18. It is perhaps described in a battle-scene in the long poem published by Ebeling in *M.A.O.G.*, XII, 2 (1938): "Bruchstücke eines politischen Propagandagedichtes aus einer assyrischen Kanzlei", col. II, 13ff., cf. 36, where the Assyrian warriors cry "Ishtar, how long!" The form-critical determination of the type of this long poem is difficult, as both its beginning and conclusion are illegible. The legible parts give an epic description of the relations between Assyrians and Kassites between Assuruballit I and Tukulti-Ninurta I (1380–1230). Perhaps we should view it in the light of what has just been said of Ps. 20 (cf. the preceding note).

19. cf. my *Det sakrale kongedömme*, pp. 47ff.; *Old Testament Essays*, Oxford (1927), pp. 143ff.

20. cf. Goppelt, *Typos*, pp. 123ff.

21. The translation "will take me up" of the American translation is possible, but unnecessary; cf. the parallels in Labat, *op. cit.*, p. 63.

22. See my commentary.

23. See my *Introduction*, I, p. 140.

24. With the following pages, compare my contribution to the *Festschrift* to Eissfeldt (1947).

25. *N.T.T.* (1944), pp. 70ff.; cf. my *Det sakrale kongedömme*, pp. 34f.

26. See, now, also H. Birkeland, "The Belief in the Resurrection of the Dead in the Old Testament", *S.T.*, III, 1, 1949 (Lund, 1950), p. 68, n. 1.

27. But see below, p. 54, and my commentary, *Isaiah II*, pp. 100, 105, and 109.

28. There is no certain confirmation of the idea that the Babylonian king was originally killed after a certain period of rule, and that the so-called *šar-pûḥi* was killed in his place. The *šar-pûḥi* is a substitute for the king and has to draw upon himself any disasters which may happen to him. It is only in exceptional circumstances that he is killed and then not because the king *must* be killed ritually, but because he is in danger of death, e.g. because of evil presages demanding his death (Labat, *op. cit.*, pp. 110, 359f.).

29. *S.E.Å.* (1945), pp. 66ff. A still later article, "Hieros gamos och underjordsvistelse", *R. Bib.* (1948), collects more material from other sources, but in my opinion does not alter the position.

30. In connection with these ideas and the exaggerations in Haldar, *Associations of Cult Prophets among the Ancient Semites* (1945), *Studies in Nahum* (1947) and *The Notion of the Desert* (1950), see Mowinckel, *He That Cometh*, Additional Note VIII.

31. cf. Hvidberg, *Den israelitiske Religions Historie* (1943), p. 170; Hooke, *Myth and Ritual*, p. 84; T. H. Robinson, *ibid.*, pp. 172ff., 183, 187f.; A. R. Johnson, *The Labyrinth*, pp. 73ff.

32. On the arguments drawn from the institution of a *šar-pûḥi*, a sham king who was somethimes killed in the ritual, cf. Mowinckel, *He That Cometh*, p. 223, n. 2.

33. See S. A. Cook, *The Old Testament, A Re-interpretation* (1936), p. 165; Engnell, *Studies*, p. 29, n. 2; Mowinckel, *He That Cometh*, p. 352, n. 2; also Jacobsen, *The Intellectual Adventure of Ancient Man*, p. 199; "It is one of the tenets of mythopoeic logic that similarity and identity merge; 'to be like' is as good as 'to be' ".

34. cf. Mowinckel, *He That Cometh*, p. 459.

35. *Acta Orientalia* (1940), pp. 11f.

36. 1 Kings 18: 27 says nothing of an égersis of Ba'al (cf. Widengren, *S.E.Å.* (1945), p. 76f. and the quotations from Dussaud, p. 77, n. 1). The mocking words of Elijah do not suppose that Ba'al is in the underworld, but only that he is sleeping. To associate this text with the Ras Shamra texts and the resurrection of Ba'al is to indulge in fantasy and to provide an example of the parallels which are often found at first sight, but which ought to be dismissed on further critical inspection. Dussaud repeats the theory in *Histoire Générale des Religions*, ed. Gorce and Mortier, vol. i (Paris, 1948), p. 365. Equally fantastic is Haldar's interpretation of Mal. 3: 1 as the god *returning from the underworld* (cf. Widengren, *op. cit.*, p. 78). The most we can say is that the phrase may be originally connected with the idea of the victorious entry of Yahweh into his temple after his combat with Chaos. It is also possible that such phrases were connected with Canaanite rites concerned with the death of Ba'al. But the question to be answered by the Old Testament scholar concerns not only the origin of the phrase but also its meaning for Malachi in the fifth century B.C. To give priority to the search for origins is to be diverted from the chief task of interpretation (as Wellhausen pointed out). The antiquarian interest of traditio-historical investigations is very great and important. The analogies in myth and ritual can in many ways illustrate the outward form of the Israelite cult, but nevertheless the pursuit of them can prove dangerous. It is worth recalling the warning of Wellhausen on the publication of Gunkel's first works on apocalyptic literature (*Skizzen und Vorarbeiten*, VI (1899), pp. 233f.); cf. Widengren, *op. cit.*, p. 80: "As I have already stressed we . . . first have to analyse the cultic motives as a preparation for a real interpretation of this and similar psalms". We must also ask whether the cultic motives found in the Psalms have the same meaning in the Israelite as in the Canaanite context. A good example of such discrimination is given by Johs. Pedersen, *Israel*, I–II, p. 548, where he develops the difference between the Israelite Levirate and similar phenomena in the laws of other Oriental nations and then adds: "This should be a warning to scholars who want to solve such problems all over the world with one single formula"; cf. also, in this connection, the words of a Roman Catholic scholar in *R.B.* (1925), p. 524, and those of Eichrodt, *Man in the Old Testament*, p. 32, n. 7.

These observations are true, *mutatis mutandis,* of the modern very interesting work on the so-called "ritual pattern" and the phenomenology of religion.

37. See the material collected in my article in the *Bertholet-Festschrift.*

38. We should also remember what A. R. Johnson says of the Israelite conception of death as a lower degree of life (*The Vitality of the Individual,* 2nd ed. pp. 88ff.).

39. On the difference between Mowinckel and myself on the conception of "death" in Isa. 53, see below, p. 54.

40. See Mowinckel, *Psalmenstudien,* I, p. 73, but also the criticisms of Birkeland in *Die Feinde des Individuums in der israelitischen Psalmenliteratur* (1933), pp. 223f. For Mowinckel's reply, see *N.T.T.* (1934), pp. 26f. We can also point out that Ps. 72: 9 mentions some "animals of the desert" which are not to be "emended away", cf. Johs. Pedersen, *Israel,* I–II, pp. 454f.; Deut. 8: 15; Isa. 34: 9–15. "Animals of the desert" can very well be placed in parallelism with "enemies". The Syriac reads "the Islands" which, like the Desert, means the rim of the earth at the frontier of Chaos (cf. my book, *Jahves Gaest* (1926), pp. 14ff. and Johs. Pedersen, *Israel,* I–II, pp. 453ff.). Widengren says that in Mesopotamia, too, the desert, the steppe, plays the rôle of the "bad land" (*S.E.Å.* (1945), p. 72). Haldar, in *The Notion of the Desert,* combines great learning with little discrimination. The description in Ps. 22 of the sufferings of the innocent man is not a description of illness, but of an *execution* (see my commentary). The Sufferer is described at the place of execution, surrounded by the demons which are thought to assemble there (cf. the material collected in my contribution to the *Bertholet-Festschrift,* where what is said of burial grounds and the underworld is in the main applicable to places of execution).

41. See the texts in Kittel, *Biblia Heb.,* 3rd edition, and my commentary. The expression, "all who go down to the dust" ("the dust" being a designation of the underworld) has a parallel in Ras Shamra I AB, V, 15f.

42. Theologically, the psalm proves that the O.T. in general did not see the significance of the suffering and death of the saviour-king. Only in Isa. 53, and the very few echoes of this poem, do we find an understanding of the ideas which became the programme of the Drama of Salvation in the New Testament. But the prophet who conceived Isa. 53 did not comprehend the meaning of the divinity of the dying saviour; cf. below, p. 67.

43. See my commentary and the passages of my *Introduction,* I, quoted in the index.

44. Widengren, *S.E.Å.* (1945), p. 80, with further references.

45. Johs. Pedersen, in *Berytus,* VI (1941), pp. 63ff. and Engnell, "The Text II K from Ras Shamra" (*R. Bib.,* 1944), pp. 1ff.

46. cf. Engnell, *The 'Ebed Yahweh Songs and the Suffering Messiah* (1948), pp. 28f.

47. cf. my *Det sakrale kongedömme*, p. 21.

48. *Det sakrale kongedömme*, pp. 78f.

49. In my *Det sakrale kongedömme*, I have attempted to draw certain limits to the theory that the psalms as a whole are to be regarded as Royal Psalms; see especially pp. 107ff.

50. *ibid.*, pp. 39 and 109. It must, however, be noted that K. Stendahl in *S.E.Å.* (1951), in an article on the meaning of *râpâ'* has made out a good case for the thesis that the word "heal" may refer to a religious, cultic reality.

51. *ibid.*, p. 58.

52. *ibid.*, pp. 58, 61.

53. cf. *Det sakrale kongedömme*, p. 36.

54. The following observations have been published in expanded form in *J.B.L.*, LXVII, 1 (1948), pp. 37ff.

55. cf. my commentary, pp. 643f.; *Det sakrale kongedömme*, p. 104. Mowinckel (*He That Cometh*, p. 83) thinks that the festival is a celebration of the entry of the Ark under David, repeated annually. This does not contradict the view that the ascension festival of the king may also be implied.

56. cf. Engnell, *Studies*, p. 35, with further references.

57. On the story of the Ark, see Rost, *Die Überlieferung von der Thronnachfolge Davids* (1926); Eissfeldt, *Introduction*, pp. 137ff.; and my *Introduction*, II, pp. 94f.

58. This interpretation of 2 Sam. 6 is to be found in Mowinckel, *Psalmenstudien*, II (1922), pp. 109ff., but, of course, it has consequences for the corresponding chapters in 1 Sam.

59. cf. above, p. 13.

60. Above, pp. 26ff., following Pedersen, Hvidberg and Engnell.

61. Goodspeed's translation. On the N.T. use of Ps. 16: 10 in Acts 2: 25–28 and 13: 35–37, see Goppelt, *Typos*, pp. 146f.

62. cf. Johs. Pedersen, *Israel*, III–IV, pp. 229f., 237ff., 524ff. He sees the probable connection between an ancient cultic song like Ps. 132 and the divine promise in 2 Sam. 7. We must note that the Story of the Ark is no direct "translation" of the ritual. Just as the Exodus Story is not *the* ritual or *the* myth, but a later epic development (cf. *Det sakrale kongedömme*, p. 15, nn. 2–3; *Introduction*, II, pp. 79ff., Engnell, *Gamla testamentet*, I, pp. 218f.), so the Story of the Ark is a "de-cultizing", an "historification". Further, certain features in Ps. 132 have no counterpart in the stories, e.g. the seeking for the ark in v. 6.

63. On such a "New Myth", see below, pp. 57ff.

## Chapter 4

1. *Culture and Conscience* (1936), pp. 101f.

2. *op. cit.*, p. 306; Breasted, *The Dawn of Conscience*, pp. 336ff.

3. *Studies*, p. 43, n. 3; cf. p. 176.

4. *Gamla testamentet*, I (1945), pp. 141f. The translation is mine.

5. *R. Bib.* (1943), pp. 74ff.

6. Mowinckel, *N.T.T.* (1944), pp. 76f.; *He That Cometh*, ch. 1, *et passim*; Sjoberg, *S.E.Å.* (1949), pp. 40f.

7. Hölscher, *Die Ursprünge der jüdischen Eschatologie* (Giessen, 1924).

8. See the very significant observations on this theme by Mowinckel, *He That Cometh*, pp. 96ff. He also stresses the important fact that the cultic experience was always a disappointment. The New Year did not fulfil the high expectations. The history of Israel, with all its disasters, ending in the downfall of the Davidic kingdom in 587, gave feelings of this kind an enormous extra force, which tended to weaken the expectations attached to the annual festival and to lay the foundation for a "futurist" hope of restoration. This, in its turn, becomes a real "eschatology" with the advent of its characteristic features—transcendence and dualism. Consequently (as Mowinckel sees clearly), the only figure then deserving the name of Messiah becomes the Son of Man. My conception will serve its purpose of describing the change—the "Gestaltwandlung"—in the figure of the Messiah through the centuries (cf. my review of Mowinckel's book in *D.T.T.* (1951), pp. 112ff. and below, pp. 73ff.).

9. We must not forget that the greatest danger lies in speaking to laymen with a fundamentalist background.

10. As is said above, I cannot accept the interpretation of this passage taken over by Noth from earlier exegetes. It is a relic from the days when the divinization of the ancient kings was thought blasphemous and it represents the artificiality of the attempts of the old orthodoxy to avoid "idolatry" and of its sister rationalism to avoid "enthusiasm".

11. On this point, Mowinckel and I differ; see Mowinckel's article, "Urmensch und Königsideologie", in *S.T.*, II, 1 (1949) and my reply, *ibid.*, III, 2. When I speak of "primeval" or "primordial" Man, I find a parallel to the discussion about the Messiah referred to in the preceding pages. Mowinckel makes an emphatic distinction between the Iranian "Urmensch", primeval Man, and the O.T. "First Created Man". I can see that the distinction is important, but I do not agree that it is absolute, as Mowinckel thinks. I regard "Adam"—the "First Created Man"—as a

variant of the type, developed in other forms in Iran, India and Scandinavia. This is the background of the following section. On the question of Cosmic Man and Man as Cosmos, see Festugière, *Les Révélations d'Hermès Trismégiste*, I (1947), pp. 92ff. I think that this description of a Hellenistic "Ymir", who determines the shape and fate of humanity, is a good proof of my assumption that the "First Man" of Genesis is a variant of the same idea. Adam also—by his disobedience to God—determines the fate of humanity. The Iranian type is regarded as the physical cause of man's fate; Adam is conceived in moral categories.

## Chapter 5

1. *Opphavet til den senjödiske forestilling om Menneskesönnen, N.T.T.* (1944), pp. 189ff. (*Acta Mowinckeliana*, pp. 29ff.). For later observations on the question, see above, p. 96, n. 11.

2. I cannot separate Mic. 5: 4 from the preceding words, as Mowinckel does in *G.T.M.M.M.*, III (1944), p. 683, and in *He That Cometh*, p. 19. The "return" referred to in 2*b* is not the return of the exiles in Babylon after 587, but an expected return of exiles to "the sons of Israel", i.e. to the northern kingdom. This agrees with the mentioning of Assur in v. 4. The only later addition I can discern in 4: 14–5: 5 is 5: 5*b*. Accordingly, the passages must be read against the background of the Assyrian dominion over Judah in the seventh century, after the defeat of Hezekiah in 701. Similarly, I do not consider it necessary to date Isa. 11: 1–9 in the early post-exilic period; cf. Johs. Pedersen, *Israel*, III–IV, p. 91, n. 1; Hammershaimb, *Some Aspects of Old Testament Prophecy*, pp. 25f. Mowinckel's rejoinder to Johs. Pedersen and Hammershaimb in *He That Cometh*, (p. 17, n. 2) only proves that there may be some uncertainty in the use of the image of the *gezaʿ*. Mowinckel now decidedly prefers the traditional pre-exilic dating of 9: 1–6 (*op. cit.*, p. 17 and pp. 102ff.). This also makes it more probable that the other poems belong to the same period. But the importance of the discussion can be exaggerated. All the oracles belong to the period of oppression which began in the middle of the eighth century and in which the capture of Jerusalem in 587 was more the culmination of a period of distress than a decisive crisis. The age from the beginning of the great westward expansion of Assyria after the accession of Tiglath-Pileser in 745 must really be regarded as the prelude to the Exile. Therefore, prophetic passages about the downfall of the Davidic dynasty may date from these early days. This way of thinking is a parallel to the "proleptic death" of the Sufferer in the Psalms of Lamentation.

3. *S.T.*, II, 1, pp. 84ff.; cf. also Sjöberg, *S.T.K.* (1950), pp. 42ff.

4. cf. *S.T.*, III, 2, pp. 152ff., and *S.T.K.* (1951), pp. 166ff.

5. The impossibility of distinguishing between "First Man" and "Man in General" is seen in Sjöberg's article (*op. cit.*, p. 43, n. 27), where he rightly repudiates Mowinckel's opinion that *'enôš* should be understood as a collective and proves that it is frequently used with an individual meaning.

6. For the criticism of Mowinckel, see *S.T.*, III, 2, 149.

7. For the description of the king, see Bertholet's commentary in Eissfeldt's *Handbuch zum Alten Testament*.

8. *N.T.T.* (1944), p. 233 (*Acta Mowinckeliana*, p. 73); cf. *S.T.*, II, pp. 71ff.; *He That Cometh*, pp. 402ff., and my article, *S.T.*, III, pp. 148ff.

9. Here Mowinckel once acknowledged the influence of the "Urmensch-myth" (*N.T.T.*, 1944, p. 196, *Acta Mowinckeliana*, p. 36). He has withdrawn this acknowledgement in *S.T.*, II, 1, p. 74; *He That Cometh*, pp. 422ff. See my observations in *S.T.*, III, 2, 1949 (Lund, 1951), p. 149.

10. cf. the analysis of Messel in *G.T.M.M.M.*, III (cf. Aelian Var. hist., 14: 30), and in *Ezechielfragen* (1945), *ad loc.* (*Skrifter, utgitt av Viden-skapsselskapet*, Oslo).

11. *Le premier homme et le premier roi*, I (1918), p. 32.

12. *S.T.*, II, 1, 1948 (Lund, 1949), p. 83.

13. See also Johs. Pedersen, *Israel*, I–II, p. 491.

14. Sjöberg, *S.T.K.* (1950), p. 39, admits that "Son of Man" is used here of the king, but denies that it is a royal title. Nevertheless, he goes so far as to admit that even this might be an allusion to the Creation myth and the primordial king, installed by God. I think that the psalm (even without the conjecture of *gannâh* instead of *kannâh* in v. 16) so abounds in allusions to the ideas of Paradise, used as descriptions of the Holy Land, that the context strongly favours the opinion that v. 18 speaks of the king of Israel as king of Paradise (see vv. 8ff. which is strongly reminiscent of the myth of the "World Tree"). Contrary to Sjöberg (*op. cit.*, p. 40, n. 16), I think this is true of Ezek. 28.

15. See *S.T.*, III, 2, 1949 (Lund, 1951), p. 152.

16. For this term, see Labat, *Le Caractère religieux*, p. 29.

17. *Hoseaboken* in *U.U.Å.* (1941), pp. 26ff. On the significance of "Fathers", see also Festugière, *Les Révélations d'Hermès Trismégiste*, I pp. 332ff. I have not seen the article of Dürr, "Heilige Vaterschaft im Antiken Orient", in *Heilige Überlieferung*, Festgabe, Tld. Fleerwegen (Münster, 1938). The Wisdom Teacher appears as Patriarch and transmits the Word of God (Festugière, *op. cit.*, pp. 335f.).

18. See Nyberg, *S.E.Å.* (1942), p. 70; on pp. 68ff. of this important treatment of the 'Ebed Yahweh of Deutero-Isaiah, Nyberg repeats and supplements his description of the Patriarch.

19. Nyberg, *op. cit.*, pp. 63–68.

## Chapter 6

1. The literature is so widespread that it seems impossible nowadays to keep a complete command of it. C. R. North, *The Suffering Servant in Deutero-Isaiah* (1948), nevertheless gives a very full, if not quite exhaustive, bibliography, as also does Curt Lindhagen in his valuable thesis, *The Servant Motif in the Old Testament* (Uppsala, 1950). North's book is supplemented by his article in *S.J.T.* III, 1950, pp. 363ff., "The Suffering Servant: Current Scandinavian Discussions", which covers the subject to October 1949. Later contributions include Mowinckel's treatment in *He That Cometh*, pp. 187–257 and a small but interesting article by E. J. Young in *The Westminster Journal of Theology* (November, 1950), pp. 19ff. The latter (apart from its untenable fundamentalist position) makes some good observations about the essential differences between Isa. 53 and the parallels from the Ras Shamra texts. It also discusses the contents of an article by J. Philip Hyatt, "The Sources of the Suffering Servant Idea", in *J.N.E.S.*, III (1944), pp. 79–96, which I have not seen, but cf. North, *op. cit.*, p. 102, n. 1, and Lindhagen, *op. cit.*, pp. 208 and 213 (notes).—See also the Supplement to my *Introduction*, I–II, 2nd ed. (1952), pp. 25 ff. on important works by Lindblom and Rowley.

The chief works under discussion in the following pages are the article of Engnell in *S.E.Å.* (1945), pp. 30–65, translated as "The 'Ebed Yahweh Songs and the Suffering Messiah in Deutero-Isaiah" in the *B.J.R.L.*, vol. 31, 1, January, 1948, and the article of Nyberg in *S.E.Å.* (1942). As usual, Engnell's work is valuable for its rich selection of literature. Finally, I may record my own latest work on the subject: the article "Herrens Tjener" in *I.R.*, II, pp. 167f.; the paper read to the Congress of Orientalists in Paris in 1948, published in *S.T.*, 1-2, see below, pp. 56ff. See also North's article in *Studies in Prophecy*, ed. H. H. Rowley (1950), and my *Introduction*, I–II (1952), *loc. cit.*

2. Engnell, *op. cit.*, p. 39. (The English edition is quoted unless otherwise stated.)

3. Lindhagen gave a good survey in *S.T.K.* (1932). My own views have been previously stated in *Jahves Tjener* (1928) and in my commentary on Isaiah (in Danish), II (1943), pp. 106 and 109, and more elaborately in I (1944), pp. viii–xi, and in *Haandbog i Kristendomskundskab*, ed. Bentzen, Feveile, Hansen, Koch, Mosbech and Plum, VIII (1945), pp. 195–201. The combination of "collective" and "individual-Messianic" interpretations, but without any connection with the person of the prophet, may be found in an article by P. Brodersen in the *Haandbog*, VIII, pp. 194–95. Engnell already made reference to his interpretation in his *Studies in Divine Kingship*, pp. 48, n. 7, and 152, n. 1. A. R. Johnson (in *The Labyrinth*, ed.

Hooke) pointed out the relation between Psalms like 89, 18, 118 and Isa. 53. The "mythological line" from Tammuz via Krt in the Ras Shamra texts was drawn by Mowinckel, *N.T.T.* (1942), pp. 24ff.; cf. *G.T.M.M.M.*, III (1944), pp. 187f. and 192–201. Hylander follows Nyberg in *Den nya kyrkosynen* (Brilioth, Fridrichsen, Hylander, Josefson and Nygren) (1945), pp. 35ff.

4. Engnell's work on this subject gives his solution to the problem in the framework of a sketch of the composition of the Book of Isaiah. This part of the work contains very much of interest, but the small space he had at his disposal enabled him to give only his general ideas of the conception without discussion, which is unfortunate as the ideas are well worth serious consideration. The so-called "traditio-historical" method is fundamental for the interpretation of the literature of the O.T. and it has been expounded in Engnell's *Gamla testamentet*, I (1945), of which we still await the second part. The most characteristic feature of it is the great attention paid to the rôle of *oral tradition*, a subject which has been discussed very intensively since the publication of the first (Swiss) edition of this book. The discussion has been presented in an admirable way by G. W. Anderson in his paper, "Some Aspects of the Uppsala School of Old Testament Study", read at the Silver Jubilee Meeting of the British Society for Old Testament Study held at Bangor in 1949, and now published in *H.T.R.*, XLIII, October, 1950, pp. 239ff. It is regrettable that the part of Engnell's paper on the Servant Songs which dealt with the composition of the Book of Isaiah has been omitted from the English version; a summary of it is therefore necessary. Engnell stresses very strongly that the witness of tradition to the *unity of the book* must have some meaning. This does not mean that he goes back to the traditionalist view of the eighth-century prophet as the "author" of the entire book, but he thinks that there are elements which combine the different parts of it and that there is also a personal, unifying link in the great collection. This link is found in the Deutero-Isaianic circle, which must have had direct contact with the disciples of the first Isaiah. Again, behind the so-called "Trito-Isaiah", he finds another circle in living contact with the Deutero-Isaianic congregation. The kernel of the book, the Deutero-Isaianic complex (44–55) is a fixed composition, belonging to the "liturgy-type" of prophetic book. Engnell follows a hint given by Gyllenberg (*S.E.Å.*, 1940, pp. 87f.; cf. Engnell's quotation, *ibid.*, 1945, p. 33, n. 6, which has unfortunately dropped out of n. 1 on p. 6 of the English version): Deutero-Isaiah is regarded as a prophetic *imitation* of a cult liturgy, a ritual for the enthronement festival.

I must emphasize that in general I accept the idea of Gyllenberg as developed by Engnell. Unhappily, I overlooked Gyllenberg's idea when I wrote my commentary; I should have been grateful to use it in my attempt to establish a closer connection between the units of the collection. Despite Mowinckel's criticism in *D.T.T.* (1946), pp. 142–68, I still think this idea is on the right lines (cf. my *Introduction*, II, p. 114). It leads to the assumption that the Servant Songs are organically connected with their context,

as I have tried to show in my commentary, and as is still strongly emphasized by Engnell (*op. cit.*, p. 9) against Mowinckel's view in *Acta Orientalia*
(1937), pp. 1ff. and *G.T.M.M.M.*, III, pp. 192ff.; cf. now, *He That Cometh*,
ch. VII, *passim*, especially in the notes. Mowinckel thinks that the Servant
Songs are a later correction of Deutero-Isaiah's earlier belief that Cyrus was
to be the Messiah. (He follows Haller, who interpreted 42: 5–7 as a Cyrus
Song; cf. Mowinckel, *op. cit.*, p. 189, n. 2.) The Songs are then referred to a
circle inside the Deutero-Isaianic circle, gathered around the memory of a
prophet later than Deutero-Isaiah. His death had shaken the circle, but, as
Isa. 53 shows, he was believed to have risen again and to be living in his
congregation and speaking to it, like Christ in the Gospel of St. John.
Mowinckel thinks that this 'Ebed Yahweh was the object of a sort of cult in
this circle. These ideas are very interesting and well-substantiated, but they
cannot be reviewed in detail here. As far as I can see, there is not sufficient
material to establish the sharp distinction between the Servant Songs and
the rest of Deutero-Isaiah which Mowinckel aims at. I do not think that he
has proved that 49: 5–6 simply describes a spiritual activity on the part of
the Servant to lead Israel back to God; he asserts that there is no idea of a
leading back of the people to Palestine (p. 192). When, however, it is
admitted that the "conversion" will also lead to a "collection" of the nations
as part of the national restoration, the Servant seems to be the instrument of
Yahweh for this task. The text does not suggest that the "collection" is not a
parallel to the expressions interpreted by Mowinckel as meaning a
"conversion" (cf. my review in *D.T.T.* (1951), pp. 112ff.).

5. When Engnell (*op. cit.*, p. 39) says that the Roman Catholic interpreters
almost without exception maintain the Messianic interpretation, his words
must be explained by a reference to Dürr, who, in the work quoted above
on Ps. 110, says that on his interpretation the "direct authorship of David
must be dropped, as *also the Messianic character of the Psalm* . . . suffers a
modification". Referring to St. Thomas, *Summa Theol.*, II, 2, qu. 174, a. 6,
and Happel, *Theol. prakt. Monatsschrift* (1906), pp. 269ff. and 335ff., he
assumes a *typological* interpretation. He also refers to Landesdorfer, *J.S.O.R.*,
9, pp. 125f. The Roman Catholic commentator Kissane, who is so enthusi-
astically praised by Engnell, does not interpret the Messianic promises as
*direct* predictions of Jesus, although he cannot be said to speak very clearly
on this subject. This has perhaps led Engnell to include him among the
exegetes who maintain the Messianic interpretation. Kissane pays attention
to the historical interpretation, but stresses the "elasticity" in the description of the Messiah in the prophetic books; and in his treatment of the
Immanuel passage, he hints at the idea that the use of the word *parthenos* in
the LXX may be due to a revelation between the time of Isaiah and the
origin of the Greek translation. That corresponds to the concluding words
of Dürr on "the law of evolution". On Ps. 110, Phythian-Adams says that
"the Psalm is a Messianic prophecy *malgré lui*" (*The Way of At-one-ment*,
1947, p. 33).

6. Engnell, *op. cit.*, p. 40.

7. Engnell refers to Murmelstein in *W.Z.K.M.* (1928), pp. 51f. Engnell (*loc. cit.*, n. 2) says that sacral kingship must be the root idea from which spring (*a*) the more or less national Messianic line of thought, not least in Israel, the most common one; (*b*) the suffering aspect; and (*c*) the "primeval man" idea, at such stages of culture when sacral kingship is non-existent, represented to a certain extent by the "prime ancestor" figure, the most typical trait of which is, in much later times, its gnosticization.

8. Much of this is stressed in opposition to Nyberg, who less one-sidedly assumes several "sources" for the Servant idea.

9. Engnell, *op. cit.*, p. 6.

10. I cannot say that I am quite convinced about Ps. 116. I still adhere to my interpretation in *Det sakrale kongedömme*, pp. 66ff., that it is not a passion, but a thanksgiving liturgy. Nyberg has called attention to the difficulty of the Aramaisms in the paper mentioned above, p. 99, n. 1.

11. I have mainly worked on the presuppositions of literary criticism, which is so strongly deprecated by Engnell. I cannot see that it is impossible to combine the traditio-historical and literary methods, as Engnell maintains (cf. *op. cit.*, p. 10, n. 5). I think a compromise is necessary; see Mowinckel, *Prophecy and Tradition*, and Widengren, "Literary and Psychological Aspects of the Hebrew Prophets", in *U.U.Å.* (1948); Lindblom's *La composition du livre de Job* (1945), p. 34; and my *Introduction*, I, pp. 102ff.— Important remarks on the significance of *oral tradition* in New Testament literary history are given by C. H. Dodd, in *According to the Scriptures* (1952), p. 29. They support the ideas of the Uppsala school without alluding to it. But on the following page Dodd also assumes, in some cases, "a common written source" between the Synoptic Gospels. This methodologically looks very sound.

12. In Babylonia, *mubassiru* was a term denoting an oracle-priest; cf. Haldar, *Associations of Cult Prophets*, 1945, p. 33. Haldar's opinions of the Hebrew word—he does not deal with Isa. 41: 27—and its synonyms seem to me somewhat adventurous. The most probable interpretation is that the *mebassêr* of 41: 27*b* is Deutero-Isaiah himself, as Mowinckel maintained in his first treatment of the Servant Songs in 1921, and still in *He That Cometh*, p. 218, n. 2, and by Begrich in his *Studien zu Deuterojesaja* (1938). In 52: 7, the *mebassêr* cannot be identical with the Messiah, but is a messenger with the good tidings that Yahweh has ascended his throne; cf. Nahum 2: 1, where he appears as a messenger calling to a feast. Accordingly, the word seems to have a cultic background, but it cannot be especially connected with the royal ideology in the O.T., and as far as I can see the same is true of Babylon, where it means the bearer of an oracle, i.e. probably something like a prophet (cf. Noth, *The Laws in the Pentateuch and Other Studies* (1966), pp. 183ff., where we have the situation but not the term). This is also supported by the context in Isa. 52: 8, where "scouts" are spoken

of; cf. Isa. 21 : 6 and Haldar, *op. cit.*, pp. 104ff., who understands this passage of the operations of a cult-prophetic congregation. This is perhaps an improvement on the usual psychological interpretation which I used in my commentary. If *mᵉbassēr* as some sort of prophet should be used as an argument for king ideology, see my later observations, p. 63.

13. See my small book, *Jahves Tjener* (1928), pp. 11 and 21f., where I have made some stylistic comparisons with Ps. 2; cf. also my *Commentary on Isaiah*, II, p. 32. Mowinckel has clearly seen the connection between prophetic and royal oracles of Call ("Motiver og stilformer i profeten Jeremias diktning", in the literary journal, *Edda*, 1926, p. 257; cf. *G.T.M.M.M.*, III, pp. 210f.).

14. This is also well described by Engnell, *op. cit.*, pp. 14f.

15. *op. cit.*, p. 15.

16. Engnell rightly refers to Östborn, *Tōrā in the Old Testament* (1945), p. 77, with a reference to the rôle of sacral kingship, the king as nòmos émpsychos; the words *ruᵃh* and *mišpāt* may also be connected with king ideology.

17. Engnell, *op. cit.*, p. 15; but see Mowinckel in *G.T.M.M.M.*, III, p. 195; *He That Cometh*, p. 190 and n. 1.

18. Engnell, *op. cit.*, n. 1.

19. Engnell, *op. cit.*, p. 16, refers in n. 1 to Wainwright, *The Sky-Religion of Egypt*, pp. 76f.

20. cf. above, pp. 45ff. At least the parallelism of king and prophet as understood by Mowinckel is also found in Accadian culture; cf. his article on the style of Jeremiah quoted above, n. 13, and his *Psalmenstudien*, III, pp. 78ff.

21. cf. above, p. 44, and Engnell, *op. cit.*, p. 16.

22. cf. *Det sakrale kongedömme*, p. 25, and the references to Widengren in n. 5.

23. Engnell here (*op. cit.*, p. 16, n. 2) refers to the article of Naor in *Z.A.W.* (1931), pp. 317ff., where Jeshurun and Jisrael are derived from the same stem as Ashera, the fertility goddess; cf. also Danell, *Studies in the Name Israel in the Old Testament* (1946), pp. 22ff. and Engnell in *Symbolae Biblicae Upsalienses* (1946), pp. 19f.

24. The idea is called a "mere suggestion"; in the Swedish original, Engnell spoke with a little more confidence. The last sentence in n. 2 on p. 16 is added in the English version, and it represents a real improvement.

25. *op. cit.*, p. 17.

26. cf. Johs. Pedersen, *Israel*, I–II, p. 527, n. 324, 1; Mowinckel, *He That Cometh*, pp. 149f.

27. cf. my commentary and Mowinckel in *G.T.M.M.M.*, III, *ad loc.*

28. cf. the express words of Engnell on p. 29: he does not derive the "pattern" from Babylon, but considers (e.g.) "the Tammuz interpretation" "an idea autochthonic to the Western Semites" (cf. below, p. 55).

29. For the different view of Mowinckel, see above, p. 101, n. 4.

30. For this literary type, see Eissfeldt, *Introduction*, pp. 55f., and my *Introduction*, I, pp. 246 and 257.

31. *op. cit.*, p. 19.

32. I did not know the special researches of Bewer on MS. Kennicott 96, quoted by Engnell; but see now Mowinckel's excursus on the passage in *He That Cometh*, Additional Note XI.

33. In my commentary, p. 80; cf. Engnell, *op. cit.*, p. 19, n. 3.

34. cf. Mowinckel, *He That Cometh*, p. 462.

35. For Mowinckel's different view, see *He That Cometh*, pp. 215ff.

36. cf. Nyberg, *S.E.Å.* (1942), p. 75; see above, p. 46.

37. When Mowinckel stresses my use of the Latin "redivivus" to suggest a "Moses reincarnate", he is exaggerating my meaning (*He That Cometh* pp. 216, 228f., especially p. 229, n. 1 *ad. fin.* I mean no more than a *new* Moses, as understood by Rowley, in *The Servant of the Lord*[2], p. 82, n. 2.

38. See *Det sakrale kongedömme*, pp. 70f.; Nyberg, *S.E.Å.* (1942), p. 75.

39. *op. cit.*, pp. 19ff.

40. Engnell refers to Torrey (*Commentary*, p. 391) and Johnson (*The Labyrinth*, pp. 77ff.) as predecessors for the contention that it is originally the king alone who can call the god "my God". This may be combined with the ideas of Alt in *Der Gott der Väter* (1929); persons of Patriarchal type were naturally those to whom the address "my God" would have been appropriate as an expression of their religious relationship.

41. Bauer and Leander (*Historische Grammatik der hebräischen Sprache*, p. 480) and Torrey consider the word an "abstractum", but of course with the usual meaning "instruction". Then the word must suddenly assume the meaning "disciple". Torrey (*op. cit.*, p. 392) thinks that this is a stylistic peculiarity of Deutero-Isaiah. I am doubtful; the transition from one meaning to the other within three lines is too abrupt.

42. This cannot be contested; cf. *S.T.*, III, 2, 1949 (Lund, 1951), p. 146, with references to Hildegard Lewy's important work on Nabunaid.

43. cf. my commentary, p. 95.

44. *Det sakrale kongedömme*, pp. 47f. and 109.

45. cf. my commentary, p. 100. There I have compared the poem with Job 19 and the descriptions of the descent into Hades in the Psalms; cf. also pp. 105 and 109. I have thus reached the same conclusions as Kissane (II, p. 175), whose commentary did not come into my hands until after the end of the German occupation of Denmark. On this question I differ from Mowinckel. *He That Cometh*, p. 200 n. 3. He thinks (cf. p. 200) that up to 53: 9, inclusive, the poet takes the standpoint of a storyteller *looking back* at the life and death of the Servant. For this view, he refers to the retrospective style of the lament for the dead and the verbal forms—perfect and imperfect consecutive. I have stressed the context of the poem as it stands in the Deutero-Isaianic collection and even if I accepted Mowinckel's conception of the tenses, I should regard the whole text as prophecy. Mowinckel considers my "context" a product of the imagination, but in n. 3 on p. 200 he adds that "his conception does not exclude the possibility that the entire picture can be an ideal picture, the realization of which *belongs to the future*". That is exactly my point (italics mine).

46. cf. Engnell, *op. cit.*, p. 23, with references to Kissane.

47. In this way, I can also accept Mowinckel's treatment of the tenses and of the retrospective view up to 53: 9. This is what I said in my commentary (p. 100) as an introduction to the song. The point on which I differ from Mowinckel is that the death in v. 8, like the death in the Psalms of Lamentation, is not yet "real death" (cf. my commentary, pp. 105 and 109). I agree with him that the prophet faces the strong *possibility* of "real death".

48. In this connection, I refer readers to the answer I gave North and which he reproduced in his article in *S.J.T.* (III, 1950), p. 378: "You say you cannot combine someone who is to come with someone who is already there. But I would answer that you have to do that in the case of the fulfilment of the prophecy. Jesus is both the Suffering Servant and the coming Christ in the Glory of the World to Come. He is so, whether you think of the Gospel narratives or in sacramental-ecclesiastical categories. I think it is theologically very interesting, methodically, that in this case we can use the fulfilment as a means of explaining the O.T. text. The Servant in Isa. II is, in my conception, the personal centre of a religious *corpus Christi*, in his life and after his death living in his circle of disciples like Jacob in the *sod* (E.VV. 'council') of his sons (Gen. 49: 6), and he has believed in his own being the future saviour of Israel. In my opinion the answer to your remark lies in the idea of 'corporate personality' applied to the prophet-founder and his disciples." I may add that North is right in supposing that I have never read H. W. Robinson's *The Cross of the Servant*, but only his article on "Corporate Personality", the ideas of which are so familiar to the pupils of Johs. Pedersen, who arrived at them and taught them quite independently. Finally, I must add that the ideas concerning the Servant's "self-consciousness" must not be confused with that of Jesus. For *the Servant has absolutely no consciousness of being Divine* (see below, p. 67, and *Introduction*, I–II, 2nd ed., Supplement, pp. 23ff.).

49. *op. cit.*, p. 24; cf. my commentary, p. 109.

50. *He That Cometh*, pp. 199ff.

51. *op. cit.*, p. 28f.

52. As we said above, this is a very balanced and sound description of method. If this had been said earlier, just as distinctly, many misunderstandings would have been avoided. At this point, the Swedish paper on the Servant gave only a compilation of parallels, which *was* very easily misunderstood.

53. cf. also Vriezen, in *O.T.S.*, VII (1950), pp. 210ff., who comes to practically the same conclusion as Engnell.

54. Engnell, *op. cit.*, p. 30, n. 6. Nyberg's interpretation is to be found in *S.E.Å.* (1942), pp. 48f. It has been accepted by Mowinckel, see *He That Cometh*, p. 200. In addition to the following observations, see my paper read to the Congress of Orientalists in Paris, 1948, printed in *S.T.*, I, 1–2 (1948), pp. 183ff.

55. cf. above, p. 100, n. 4.

56. cf. above, p. 12; Johs. Pedersen, *Israel* III–IV, pp. 401ff., 408ff., V. d. Leeuw, *Phänomenologie der Religion* (1933), p. 344. (E.T., p. 367).

57. Here, we have a genuine feature of "typological interpretation"; the "antitype" is not analogous to, but also different from and greater than, the "type" (cf. Daniélou, *Sacramentum futuri* (1950), *passim*; Goppelt, *Typos*, p. 44, the notes).

58. I think there is a pointer here against Mowinckel's refusal to allow that the preaching of Deutero-Isaiah is "eschatological" (*He That Cometh*, pp. 140ff., 149ff.). In my opinion, his definition of this conception suffers from the same narrowness as his definition of "Messiah".

59. cf. above, pp. 31 ff. and Daniélou, *op. cit.*, pp. 132ff.

60. cf. Mowinckel, *op. cit.*, pp. 250ff., with the qualification that I identify the Servant and the prophet.

61. A result of thoughts on the difference between the "Old" and the "New" is the predicate of God in the synagogue prayer *lᵉel baruk* as '*Oseh hᵃdasot*.

62. I do not dispute the idea of the king being identified with the tree of life (cf. Widengren, in *R. Bib.* (1943), pp. 6off.). I think that Ezek. 31 and Dan. 4 are clear Old Testament expressions of the idea (cf. my commentary on Daniel, 2nd ed., on Dan. 4). This is a necessary supplement to my observations in *Det sakrale kongedömme*, pp. 35 and 24ff.

63. cf. his latest treatment in *He That Cometh*, pp. 80, 161, n. 3, and Additonal Notes IV and VII.

64. cf. my commentary, pp. 101f., 104f.

65. *Theology* (1926), pp. 3ff.

66. Engnell refers to Kissane on Isa. 53: 6f. and E. O. James, *Origins of Sacrifice* (1937), p. 207. James does not regard the Servant as the Messiah and his remarks are not quite clear—obviously, because he is aware of the great uncertainty of the whole question.

67. cf. also, Mowinckel's observations in *He That Cometh*, pp. 202f.: "In Israel silence and stillness (as contrasted with the 'noise' of sinners and of the powers of chaos) became to some extent the typical religious attitude, a mark of piety and uprightness, the attitude which was characteristic of the ideal of humility"; cf. *T. T.* (1932), pp. 199ff.

68. He rightly notes that in reality it is no emendation.

69. *op. cit.*, p. 58.

70. cf. Job 17: 3.

71. *op. cit.*, p. 37, n. 1, but see now Birkeland's very important article on this subject in *S. T.*, III, 1, 1949 (Lund, 1950).

72. *He That Cometh*, pp. 234ff.

73. cf. Goppelt, *Typos*, p. 46. Goppelt also finds priestly features. He adduces in favour of this opinion 53: 4ff.: the Servant sacrifices himself. Whether his intercession (53: 12) and his proclamation of the Torah also can be called priestly functions is less certain. These ideas are also connected with the prophets. Another aspect which might also be mentioned is the "shepherd ideology". There is perhaps a reminiscence of this in 53: 6 (cf. Engnell, *op. cit.*). This is a *royal* feature (cf. Goppelt, *Typos*, p. 104), which has influenced Mark 14: 24 through Zech. 9: 11. The most interesting text of this kind is John 10: 11f., where this feature of king-ideology is the background of the idea of vicarious suffering—a strong indication of the fact that the wholesale rejection of the "Uppsala ideology" is more premature than many of the arguments of the School. The Shepherd feature is also used in the New Testament picture of the Son of Man (cf. Goppelt, *op. cit.*, p. 105; Luke 19: 10; Matt. 25: 32-4; cf. Ezek. 34: 17).

74. "Historicism" and "historistic" are, therefore, bad slogans to use as arguments in a debate on Deutero-Isaiah. The Old Testament as a whole is "historistic".

75. In other situations, we see prophets making a practical application of cultic poetry, in that they understand it more "literally" than is usual in daily life. An example of this is Isaiah's "pacifism"; cf. my article in *R.H.P.R.* (1930), pp. 499ff.

76. The figure cannot be regarded as an absolutely "futuristic" idea. It would be incompatible with the manifest "reality" and "actuality" of all the *dramatis personae* in Deutero-Isaiah's ritual drama.—On the appropriateness of the term "autobiographical" in this case, see my remarks in my *Introduction*, II, 2nd ed., 1952, Appendix p. 24.

77. cf. his polemic against Mowinckel in his article *op. cit.*, p. 15, n. 1. Engnell claims that Mowinckel must prove that the forms in 42: 1ff. are "disintegrated" before they can be used of a prophet. That, however, is very probable *a priori*, because Old Testament literature in general (and not only the Psalms of which I have spoken in a similar connection in *Det sakrale kongedömme*, p. 58), and Deutero-Isaiah in particular, is "late" literature compared with Mesopotamian and Egyptian productions. Further, reference may be made to the example of Jeremiah (cf. above, p. 103, n. 13, 20). His inaugural vision is in the "royal" style, therefore the parallel passages 42: 1ff. and 49: 1ff. may—and must—be explained in the same way. We can also point to the so-called monologues of Jeremiah (cf. my *Introduction*, I, p. 164), where regular psalms of lamentation are used as "confessions" of the prophet. These descriptions of the "suffering innocent" are used here not of the king, but of the prophet.

78. cf. above, p. 44.

79. *op. cit.*, p. 18, n. 4; cf. above, p. 53.

80. cf. Lindhagen's survey; also, *Det sakrale kongedömme*, pp. 70f.

81. cf. *S.E.Å.* (1942), p. 75; cf. above, p. 45.

82. cf. above, pp. 31ff.

83. Especially in his book, *Mose* (1922), and his *Geschichte des israelitisch-jüdischen Volkes*, I (1924), pp. 76ff.; II (1932), pp. 67f.

84. cf. above, pp. 26ff. In my too exaggerated claim that *all* psalms of suffering should be explained as royal psalms, there was some truth, but the possibility that *not* all these psalms are to be understood as royal psalms (e.g. that they are expressions of the disintegration and democratization of the original pattern) must make the assumption more hypothetical. And at all events, we must remember that we cannot move with certainty from the Old Testament to the original material; cf. what has often been said about its being impossible that the Tammuz ideology was a conscious thought of Deutero-Isaiah.

85. Engnell's treatment is too concise. On 42: 7, he says that the royal ideology lies behind the healing of the blind and the liberation of the prisoners. But in 49: 9, the same metaphors are connected with the liberation and return of Israel.

86. cf. the use of the word in Goppelt, *Typos*, p. 148.

87. In the Deuteronomic literature Moses is a sort of preparation for the 'Ebed Yahweh of Deutero-Isaiah. He lacks only the "universalist" features, since he is suffering for Israel, not for the "many".

88. cf. Dürr, *Ursprung und Ausbau der israelitisch-jüdischen Heilandserwartung*, pp. 125f.; Engnell, *Studies in Divine Kingship*, pp. 35f., 66f.

89. cf. above, pp. 60f.; Widengren, *Religionens värld*, pp. 213–26; and see *Det sakrale kongedömme*, p. 112, where I have again noted that the position of intercessor is also occupied by prophets and patriarchs.

## Chapter 7

1. *S.E.Å.* (1942), pp. 79f.

2. *Die Verkündigung vom leidenden Gottesknecht aus Jes. 53 in der griechischen Bibel* (1934), pp. 125ff.

3. Johs. Pedersen, *Israel*, III–IV, pp. 662f. (italics mine); cf. also Goppelt, *Typos*, p. 126: "In der Gottesknechtweissagung klingt zusammen, was die ganze Schrift über die Propheten, Könige und Gerechten berichtet und über ihre künftigen Gegenbilder weissagt; Der Christus muss leiden, sterben und auferstehen"; and cf. also Goppelt's reference to Otto, *Reich Gottes und Menschensohn*, p. 210, emphasizing that the Old Testament fulfilment is not an expression of "blind fatality", but of a necessity founded on the relations between God and Man revealed in Holy Scripture.

4. *Det sakrale kongedömme*, p. 119; cf. also Engnell, *Gamla testamentet*, I, pp. 147ff.

5. cf. my contribution to *Haandbog i Kristendomskundskab*, VIII, p. 199, my *Jesaja*, I, p. x, and my article in *I.R.*

6. cf. the "phenomenological parallel" to this conception in the New Testament described by Goppelt, *Typos*, p. 148.

## Chapter 8

1. This is more elaborately described in *He That Cometh*.

2. In a very friendly review of the Swiss edition of this book, E. J. Young rejects this thesis. The rise of eschatology is due, he maintains, to "a special revelation to Israel" (*The Westminster Theological Journal* (1949), p. 190). I do not see that these views are alternatives; the historical experiences of Israel are God's means of revelation.

3. On the question of dating, see above, pp. 39f.

4. cf. above, pp. 49f.

5. In this connection, I quoted some pointed words by Hempel which briefly summarize the contents of the present book: "It is not the earthly king in whose blessed government God's dominion should be realized (but is not) who appears as the bearer of grace, but 'Man' in contrast to the animal powers. When the proclamation of the king as Son of God is the primitive form of 'Messianic Prophecy', life, dominion and victory being

promised to the Ruler, then the definite turning into eschatology of this
promise is completed, but in such a way that in this proclamation the
dominion of God, attacked by the 'Animals' and their 'Blasphemy', is
re-established." On New Testament use of Dan. 7, see C. H. Dodd, *According
to the Scriptures*, pp. 67ff.

6. cf. my commentary on the Psalms (1939), p. 13; Kittel, *Die hellenistische
Mysterien religion und das Alte Testament*, and above all, Bousset's and
Gunkel's epoch-making works. On the theological appreciation of this
material, see the remarks of Mowinckel in *He That Cometh*, pp. 445ff.

7. On the following observations, I refer to Daniélou, *Sacramentum futuri*,
especially pp. 155ff., where in many cases the typological interpretation is
seen to return to the ancient Creation mythology (cf. pp. 163, 168).

8. Probably many people will reproach me for falling back into "typological" exegesis. I do not regard the suggestion as a reproach. It is important to define our terms. We must make it clear that the "typological conception" (according to Torm, *Neutestamentliche Hermeneutik*, this is different
from typological exegesis) must always be considered an interpretation of
faith. When, for example, the New Testament writers use this sort of
interpretation in their study of the Old Testament, we cannot take it that
they are giving us the scientifically correct answers to the problems of
the original text. Nor can we suppose that the Old Testament writers were
consciously giving prefigurations of Jesus Christ. On the other hand,
phenomenology can point out parallel phenomena, and such parallels
can be interpreted by faith as type and anti-type. As Torm says, between
historical parallels there is a profound connection founded on the fact that
"history repeats itself". We often find, especially in the history of religions,
a profound spiritual relationship between personalities and events of
different ages. The same spiritual powers are always at work, the same
fight is perpetually waged between Good and Evil, with increasing
animosity.

According to the fundamental belief of the New Testament, history
exhibits a growing development of revelation, an ever richer self-develop-
ment of God, confronted by ever more powerful explosions of the powers of
Evil in Man. This being so, the phenomenology of religion and the interpretation of faith overlap to a considerable extent. In this connection, it is
always important to emphasize, with Torm, that the Old Testament type
of central importance is that of the Innocent Sufferer in the Psalms and the
Prophets (Pss. 22, 69; Isa. 53, *et al*. Cf. on this subject C. H. Dodd, *According
to the Scriptures*, pp. 96–103.). Torm stresses that, in such passages, Jesus
found a description of the ideal which according to the will of God he had
to realize. Such passages were regarded as "promises" of Christ. In a
similar way, Rowley (*The Biblical Doctrine of Election*, 1950, p. 160, n. 1)
speaks of "the pattern of Salvation reflected in the Old Testament revelation of God", but refuses to assume "prefiguration of New Testament
events and teachings". He takes the view that "they were a revelation of

God and that the same God revealed himself in the New Testament events".

The book by Daniélou, often referred to, attempts to show that the typological exegesis of the ancient Church started from a typology already incipient in the Old Testament and continued it as it was maintained by Judaism in its eschatologization of the "types". The Church added as its own, the idea of the *realization* of the types in Christ, the actual fulfilment, expressed in the *hodie* of Luke 23: 43. The important feature of Daniélou's treatment is that he emphasizes that the typological exegesis of antiquity (in contrast to allegory) accepts the literal, historical meaning of the Old Testament. He therefore comes very near to the view of Torm mentioned above. As far as I can see, our task is to ascertain whether, starting from our historical, scientific conception of Old Testament History and Religion, as the New Testament and Primitive Church started from *their* historical conceptions, we can read the Old Testament in a manner similar to theirs. We cannot expect to accept all their *results*; but we may adapt their "pattern" to the claims of our methods.

The sort of typology advocated by Torm and described by Daniélou has been adapted to the Old Testament Promise and Fulfilment by F. Buhl in *De Messianske Forjaettelser* (1894) with reference to the incipient typology in the Old Testament itself; see my article on "The Old Testament in the New Covenant", in *Hervormde Teologiese Studies* (Pretoria, November 1950), also printed in Danish in *Bibelsyn* (1951). See also Eichrodt, *Israel in der Weissagung des Alten Testaments* (1951).

There seems to be a growing tendency to revive typological exegesis. In this respect the book of Goppelt was a pioneer work; other expositions are mentioned in Daniélou's bibliography (where, incidentally, Phythian-Adam's *The Way of At-one-ment* has become "The Day of Atonement"!) There is still much work to be done and caution is necessary. When we try to regenerate and modernize typological exegesis, we must not forget that the historical understanding of the Old Testament in our own age must be respected, as in the Early Church their historical understanding, *which we cannot accept*, was the starting point. The *descriptions* of ancient typology, as given by Goppelt and Daniélou, are not enough; we must work out our own typology in fidelity to our historical approach.—On the New Testament understanding of Old Testament Apocalyptic, C. H. Dodd, *According to the Scriptures* (1952), p. 73, has some very good remarks.

9. See also Hans Walter Wolff, *Jes. 53 im Urchristentum* (3rd ed., 1952).

10. This rule is strongly stressed both by Goppelt and Daniélou, and it contains the important truth which prevents our equating the Testaments. *Allegory*, which Daniélou proves to be a method foreign to the main tradition of the Early Church, entering the tradition from Philo, tends to make this equation and to substitute psychology for history, by turning Old Testament events and subjects into symbols of the movements of the souls of the pious.

11. See an article by Sören Holm in the Copenhagen *Gads Danske Magasin* (1947), in which (pp. 381ff.), as part of a review of Bultmann's *Offenbarung und Heilsgeschichte* (1943), he comments on our problem in these terms: "To attain a full understanding of the extent of Bultmann's *Entmythologisierung*, it is necessary to put the question whether this means the eliminating of every form of metaphysics, of the belief in the reality of the religious object outside the human consciousness". Holm thinks that Bultmann has not distinguished clearly between metaphysics in this sense and mythology. A piece of cosmological myth is admittedly a piece of poetry, but it is also a piece of metaphysics. Here, Bultmann's analysis is not completely clear. It is not possible to relegate "mythology" to the rubbish-heap. On the contrary, *Entmythologisierung* is quite impossible. "What is superhuman can usually only be spoken of in the metaphorical picture language of myth." (Mowinckel, *He That Cometh*, p. 181). The solution seems to lie in a working method which tries to interpret the mythological concepts in the light of the religious motives underlying them. For this purpose, the comparative method of the Phenomenology of Religion may be of assistance.

# INDEX OF BIBLICAL PASSAGES

# INDEX OF AUTHORS